Celebrating
the Newly Renovated
Salt Lake Temple

Celebrating
the Newly Renovated
Salt Lake Temple

Mary Jane Woodger
& Mark D. Ogletree

CFI
An imprint of Cedar Fort, Inc.
Springville, Utah

© 2025 Mary Jane Woodger & Mark Ogletree
All rights reserved.

No part of this book may be reproduced in any form whatsoever, whether by graphic, visual, electronic, film, microfilm, tape recording, or any other means, without prior written permission of the publisher, except in the case of brief passages embodied in critical reviews and articles.

This is not an official publication of The Church of Jesus Christ of Latter-day Saints. The opinions and views expressed herein belong solely to the author and do not necessarily represent the opinions or views of Cedar Fort, Inc. Permission for the use of sources, graphics, and photos is also solely the responsibility of the author.

Paperback ISBN 13: 978-1-4621-4877-6
eBook ISBN 13: 978-1-4621-4878-3

Published by CFI, an imprint of Cedar Fort, Inc.
2373 W. 700 S., Suite 100, Springville, UT 84663
Distributed by Cedar Fort, Inc., www.cedarfort.com

Library of Congress Cataloging Number: 2025930015

Cover design by Shawnda Craig
Cover design © 2025 Cedar Fort, Inc.
Edited and Typeset by Liz Kazandzhy

Printed in the United States of America

10 9 8 7 6 5 4 3 2 1

Printed on acid-free paper

Contents

Foreword 1

Introduction 3
   My Salt Lake Temple Odyssey 5

The Building and Renovation of the Salt Lake Temple 13
   "However Long and Hard the Road" 15
   James Campbell Livingston: Laying the Foundation of a Great Work 20
   John R. Moyle's Long Walk to the Temple 27
   The Building of the Salt Lake Temple 32
   "The Temple and Your Spiritual Foundation" 45

Principles and Doctrines of the Temple 47
   The Holy of Holies and the Salt Lake Temple 49
   The Revelation on the Priesthood Received in the Temple 67
   Writing *Jesus the Christ* in the Salt Lake Temple 77
   The Security of the Sealing Power of the Priesthood 81
   Christ's Appearance to Lorenzo Snow in the Temple 91

Patrons' Personal Experiences in the Salt Lake Temple 99
   Baby Born in the Salt Lake Temple 101
   "All Will Be Well Because of Temple Covenants" 103
   Testimony-Building Experiences in the Salt Lake Temple 104
   Great-Grandma Allen's Temple Recommend 113
   The Salt Lake Temple: Home 118
   You Have Never Been Alone 126
   The Grandaddy of Them All: The Salt Lake Temple 129
   "It Brings Peace to My Heart" 133

Salt Lake Temple Workers' Experiences 135
   Holiness Is the House of the Lord 137
   John R. Winder: A Blessing in the Temple 144
   Salt Lake Temple Reflections 151
   Working in the Salt Lake Temple 155
   The Salt Lake Temple: Refuge and Refinement 161
   At the Recommend Desk 167
   Memories of the Salt Lake Temple 173
   "Marrying Ned" Winder: Legendary Sealer 179

Looking Forward 187
   Touching the Temple 189
   A Proud Monument of the Saints' Faith, Perseverance, and Industry 193

About the Authors 207

Foreword

Mark D. Ogletree & Mary Jane Woodger

WITH THE RENOVATION OF THE SALT LAKE TEMPLE TO "ENHANCE, refresh, and beautify the temple and its surrounding grounds,"[1] this commemorative compilation celebrates the rededication and reopening of the Salt Lake Temple. This volume celebrates the history, heritage, and spirit of this magnificent edifice. In creating this volume, we hope that Latter-day Saints will come to know and love the Salt Lake Temple and feel a connection to this iconic sacred building, even if they never visit it themselves.

In celebrating the reopening and rededication of the Salt Lake Temple, this compilation shares experiences that several Latter-day Saints have had while attending this holy temple. It also relates various historical events experienced within its walls by Latter-day Saints of the past. In sharing the teachings and testimonies of these faithful authors and temple patrons, and with quotes from Church leaders and the scriptures, we hope this compilation will inspire Latter-day Saints worldwide who identify the Salt Lake Temple as the headquarters of The Church of Jesus Christ of Latter-day Saints.

In his dedicatory prayer in 1893, President Wilford Woodruff envisioned what patrons would experience in the Salt Lake Temple: "O Lord, we pray Thee to bless and sanctify the whole of this block or piece of ground on which these buildings stand, with the surrounding walls and fences, the walks, paths and ornamental beds, also the trees, plants, flowers and shrubbery that grow in its soil; may they bloom and blossom and become exceedingly beautiful and fragrant; and may Thy Spirit dwell in the midst thereof, that this plot of ground may be a place of rest and peace, for holy meditation and inspired thought."[2]

This volume chronicles Latter-day Saints who have experienced what was promised in this dedication as they share their sacred feelings and personal experiences associated with the Salt Lake Temple.

Notes

1. "Plans Unveiled for Salt Lake Temple Renovation," Apr. 19, 2019, newsroom.ChurchofJesusChrist.org.
2. "Dedicatory Prayer: Salt Lake Temple, 6 April 1893," The Church of Jesus Christ of Latter-day Saints, accessed Oct. 2, 2024, https://www.churchofjesuschrist.org/temples/details/salt-lake-temple/prayer/1893-04-06.

Introduction

My Salt Lake Temple Odyssey

Richard O. Cowan

Perhaps more than with any other temple, the story of the Salt Lake Temple is intertwined with the history of the Church in general. Its location at Church headquarters has meant that this temple has fulfilled some unique functions and has been the site of some very special spiritual experiences. The Salt Lake Temple has also played an important role in my own personal spiritual odyssey at a number of key points. Hence, this account blends my own impressions of the temple with insights from my background as a scholar of Latter-day Saint temples. Being visually impaired (I became totally blind at about the turn of the century), I perceived the Salt Lake Temple and most everything else in a different way than did most people.

During my childhood in Southern California, our family typically made vacation trips to Salt Lake City, where both of my parents had grown up. On one of these trips, when I was a deacon, my parents arranged for my sister and me to participate in baptisms for the dead. As I entered the Salt Lake Temple for the first time, I sensed that I was in a holy and historic place, and I felt close to the Lord and to the pioneers who had sacrificed so much to build it. I was baptized for 121 persons, so as a young boy, I felt thoroughly immersed! As I look back on that event, I am struck by how different it was from today's typical baptism and confirmation experience. During recent decades, the growing interest among young people in participating in temple service has necessarily brought limitations on how many ordinances an individual proxy can perform at a given time. Obviously, those restrictions did not apply during the 1940s. The procedure for performing the baptismal and confirmation ordinances has also become much more efficient. When I was a young man, I climbed up dripping wet after each baptism to sit in a chair mounted on the edge of the font to be confirmed. I then got back down into the water for the next baptism. Today, a proxy is typically baptized for one person after another while remaining in the font. Then, after dressing in dry clothing, the proxy is confirmed in a separate location. Though the ordinances themselves have not changed, the more efficient procedures allow patrons to accomplish much more during the same period of time.

When I was called to serve as a missionary, I was endowed in the Salt Lake Temple as part of my Missionary Home experience. The Missionary Home had been established in 1925 to provide a brief orientation for outgoing missionaries. The decision to make the endowment a regular part of this orientation was based in part on the petition in the dedicatory prayer of the Kirtland Temple that God's "servants may go forth from this house [the temple] armed with [His] power, and that [His] name may be upon them" (Doctrine and Covenants 109:22). In earlier decades, when almost no temples were located outside of the Intermountain West, the Salt Lake Temple accounted for a much larger percentage of ordinances Churchwide, especially for the living. Therefore, my experience of being endowed there as a missionary was quite typical. However, as temples began to "dot the earth," an ever-smaller number of missionaries came to Salt Lake unendowed. Furthermore, when the Missionary Training Center (MTC) was established adjacent to Brigham Young University (BYU) in 1976, missionaries began to attend the Provo Temple.

Attending temple preparation classes was not the norm when I was preparing to receive my endowment. I therefore did not know what to expect during my visit. Still, I experienced a feeling of awe as I passed through the series of impressive ordinance rooms in the historic Salt Lake Temple and received the blessings promised there.

During my recent research, I was surprised to learn that the plan for the Salt Lake Temple was not revealed all at once. In 1854 architect Truman O. Angell published a description of the future temple. As with the Kirtland and Nauvoo temples, the interior of the Salt Lake Temple would consist almost entirely of two large meeting halls with elliptical ceilings, one above the other; four small rooms in the basement would be devoted to presenting the endowment.[1]

The temple's exterior walls were nearing completion in the mid-1880s when Church leaders considered significant changes in the plans for the yet-unconstructed interior. In 1884 Truman O. Angell Jr., who was assisting his elderly father, proposed that the Salt Lake Temple should follow the pattern that Presidents Young and Taylor had already approved for Logan and Manti: There would be only one assembly room, on the upper floor. The temple's main floor would contain spacious rooms for presenting the endowment, while an intermediate floor would provide smaller council rooms for the use of Church leaders and other priesthood groups. This plan would accommodate 300 persons in the endowment sessions—more than twice the number that could be served in the basement under the original arrangement.[2] These changes were consistent with President Young's 1860 instruction that the temple would not be designed for general meetings but rather for the endowment—for the organization and instruction of the priesthood.[3] Thus, even the developing design of the Salt Lake Temple reflected the Saints' unfolding understanding of temple functions. The final plans for the temple appear to have been drawn under President Wilford Woodruff's direction by Joseph Don Carlos Young, who became temple architect in early 1888 and architect of the Church in April 1890—just three years before the temple's completion.[4] Hence, all the work on the temple's interior was accomplished during the last few years of construction.

During my session in the Salt Lake Temple, the endowment was presented by live temple workers, as it had been from the beginning. Over the years, I witnessed the shift from the live presentation to audio recordings. Then, in 1955, films were introduced, beginning with the first "overseas temple" in Switzerland. When the Manti Temple closed for renovation in 2021, it was the last temple presenting the "live endowment." Today, rather than "progressing" from room to room as I had done in the Salt Lake Temple, patrons in almost all temples now receive the endowment in just one or two rooms.

In 1961, when I started teaching at BYU, Provo was in the Salt Lake Temple district. Before the I-15 freeway was completed along the Wasatch Front during the 1970s, our only route to the temple was taking State Street through one town after another with all their traffic and stoplights. While making that long drive back then, we would never have believed that one day we would be passing a dozen other temples on the way to the Salt Lake Temple: two in Provo and South Jordan and one in Orem, Lindon, Saratoga Springs, American Fork, Lehi, Draper, West Jordan, and Taylorsville (at the time of this writing). When I was called to serve in a BYU stake, I learned that the campus stakes were assigned to the Manti Temple. Hence, attending the temple involved a much greater time commitment than today, whether we were going north or south.

Before I served my mission, missionary groups were given tours of the Salt Lake Temple from top to bottom following their first endowment session. Then later on, missionaries met in the temple with a General Authority who answered their questions after the session. When I served, we didn't have either of these experiences for some reason, but I have had them since. On one occasion, following an endowment session in the Salt Lake Temple, BYU's religion faculty met with Elder Harold B. Lee, who answered our questions about the temple and offered inspired counsel. Hugh Nibley, a noted Latter-day Saint scholar, met with us on several occasions, generally in the Manti Temple, to share his insights, particularly on ancient temples and temple work.

In 1969 I was granted permission to have my tour of the Salt Lake Temple. I gained a greater appreciation for the features of this wonderful building, such as the murals in the endowment rooms and the architectural details in the large priesthood assembly room. We even went out on the roof of the temple. My vision was a bit better then, and I remember how short the towers looked from the roof ridgeline.

As part of this experience, we also visited the council room of the First Presidency and the Quorum of the Twelve Apostles. Because it is located at Church headquarters, the Salt Lake Temple, and particularly this room, plays a unique and significant role in Church governance.

The First Presidency sits in chairs at the front of the room, and the Quorum of the Twelve sits in chairs arranged in a semicircle facing the First Presidency. As I sat in one of the chairs, I humbly marveled at the privilege of being in that sacred place.

I recall hearing accounts affirming that during the council's weekly meetings, each person in the room is asked to share his thoughts freely as the group prayerfully seeks a consensus. In His great revelation on Church organization, the Lord instructed that these quorums' decisions "must be by the unanimous voice of the same; that is, every member in each quorum must be agreed to its decisions" (Doctrine and Covenants 107:27). "The requirement of unanimity provides a check on bias and personal idiosyncrasies," explained President James E. Faust. "It ensures that God rules through the Spirit, not man through majority or compromise."[5] Concerning the importance of unanimity, then-Elder Russell M. Nelson testified, "The calling of 15 men to the holy apostleship provides protection for us as members of the Church. Why? Because decisions of these leaders must be unanimous. Can you imagine how the Spirit needs to move upon 15 men to bring about unanimity?" Then, after becoming the prophet, President Nelson stated, "In our meetings, the majority never rules! We listen prayerfully to one another and talk with each other until we are united. Then when we have reached complete accord, the unifying influence of the Holy Ghost is spine-tingling! No member of the First Presidency or Quorum of the Twelve would ever leave decisions for the Lord's Church to his own best judgment!"[6]

These decisions have included such matters as ordaining and setting apart new Presidents of the Church, appointing General Authorities, creating new missions and stakes, and approving Church programs. Notable examples include the 1952 decision to build temples overseas, the determination in 1976 to add what we now know as sections 137 and 138 to the scriptural canon, and the 1978 revelation extending the priesthood to all worthy males (Official Declaration 2). Reflecting on these weekly meetings in the temple, President Spencer W. Kimball, serving as an Apostle at the time, affirmed that those who could witness the prophet's wisdom in reaching decisions would surely believe he was inspired: "To hear him [the prophet] conclude important new developments with such solemn expressions as 'the

Lord is pleased'; 'that move is right'; 'our Heavenly Father has spoken,' is to know positively."[7]

The Salt Lake Temple underwent a thorough renovation in the early 1960s. I remember the unusual experience of dressing in a temporary locker room located in the basement of the nearly completed North Visitors' Center and then walking southeast through a tunnel into the temple's basement for the endowment session. I have always sought to know just where I was in the building, as this helps me feel better oriented. The upward movement during the session added to my sense of progression back into God's presence.

I also followed the 2020s renovation of the Salt Lake Temple in depth. I have examined by touch one of the ninety-eight base isolators on which the temple will "float," allowing it to remain relatively stable during an earthquake. I was interested to discover that the baptistry where I was baptized years ago will be the site of new endowment presentation rooms, while two baptistries will be located in the new north addition.

Initially, Church leaders had hoped to preserve and enhance the Salt Lake Temple's historic murals. But rather than being painted on canvas, they had been painted directly on the lath and plaster walls. By the time the renovation project had passed its first year, it became increasingly evident that completely preserving the murals would be impossible. Along with many others, I was disappointed at this news but certainly understood the problem and was grateful that many other architectural details of the temple would be preserved or replicated.

President Nelson toured the construction site on Saturday, May 22, 2021. While there, he recorded part of his message for the October general conference: "As I examine the craftsmanship of this entire building, I marvel at what the pioneers accomplished." He then observed, "These many decades later, however, if we examine the foundation closely, we can see the effects of erosion, gaps in the original stonework, and varying stages of stability in the masonry. Now as I witness what modern engineers, architects, and construction experts can do to reinforce that original foundation, I am absolutely amazed. Their work is astonishing!"[8] He then challenged all members of the Church to examine and strengthen their own spiritual foundations.

Over the years, as I have left the Salt Lake Temple's celestial room and entered the large central hallway, I have often thought of President Lorenzo Snow's description of his glorious meeting with the Savior there when he became President of the Church. President Snow described what happened: "It was right here that the Lord Jesus Christ appeared to me at the time of the death of President Woodruff. He instructed me to go right ahead and reorganize the First Presidency of the Church at once and not wait as had been done after the death of the previous presidents, and that I was to succeed President Woodruff. . . . He stood right here, about three feet above the floor. It looked as though He stood on a plate of solid gold."[9] Many marvelous spiritual experiences have been linked with this temple over the years.

Without question, my Salt Lake Temple odyssey extending over three-quarters of a century has enriched me personally. I have gained a broader understanding of this temple's role in the ongoing work of the latter-day Church, and my contacts with this marvelous historic building have certainly strengthened my own life, particularly spiritually.

Notes

1. Truman O. Angell, "The Temple," *Deseret News*, Aug. 17, 1854, 2.
2. C. Mark Hamilton, *The Salt Lake Temple: A Monument to a People* (University Services, 1983), 55–57.
3. Brigham Young, in *Journal of Discourses*, 8:203.
4. Truman O. Angell Jr. to John Taylor, Apr. 28, 1885, and Angell Sr. to Taylor, Mar. 11, 1885, quoted in Hamilton, *Salt Lake Temple*, 54–57.
5. Quoted in Sheri L. Dew, *Prophets See Around Corners* (Deseret Book, 2023), 36.
6. Quoted in Dew, *Prophets See Around Corners*, 36.
7. Spencer W. Kimball, ". . . To His Servants the Prophets," *Instructor*, Aug. 1960, 257.
8. Russell M. Nelson, "The Temple and Your Spiritual Foundation," *Liahona*, Nov. 2021, 93.
9. LeRoi C. Snow, "An Experience of My Father's," *Improvement Era*, Sept. 1933, 677, 679.

PART 1

THE BUILDING AND RENOVATION OF THE SALT LAKE TEMPLE

"However Long and Hard the Road"

President Jeffrey R. Holland[1]

ON 28 JULY 1847, FOUR DAYS AFTER HIS ARRIVAL IN THAT VALLEY, Brigham Young stood upon the spot where now rises the magnificent Salt Lake Temple and exclaimed to his companions: "Here [we will build] the Temple of our God!"[2]

Its grounds would cover an eighth of a square mile, and it would be built to stand through eternity. Who cares about the money or stone or timber or glass or gold they don't have? So what that seeds are not even planted and the Saints are yet without homes? Why worry that crickets will soon be coming—and so will the United States Army? They just marched forth and broke ground for the most massive, permanent, inspiring edifice they could conceive. And they would spend forty years of their lives trying to complete it.

The work seemed ill-fated from the start. The excavation for the basement required trenches twenty feet wide and sixteen feet deep, much of it through solid gravel. Just digging for the foundation alone required nine thousand days of labor. Surely someone must have said, "A temple would be fine, but do we really need one this big?" But they kept on digging. Maybe they believed they were "laying the foundation of a great work." In any case they worked on, "not weary in well-doing."

And through it all Brigham Young had dreamed the dream and seen the vision. With the excavation complete and the cornerstone ceremony concluded, he said to the Saints assembled:

> I do not like to prophesy much, . . . But I will venture to guess that this day, and the work we have performed on it, will long be remembered by this people, and be sounded as with a trumpet's voice throughout the world. . . . Five years ago last July I was here, and saw in the spirit the Temple. [I stood] not ten feet from where we have laid the chief corner stone. I have not inquired what kind of a temple we should build. Why? Because it was [fully] represented before me.[3]

But as Brigham Young also said, "We never began to build [any] temple without the bells of hell beginning to ring."[4] No sooner was the foundation work finished than Albert Sidney Johnston and his United States troops set out for the Salt Lake Valley intent on war with "the Mormons." In response President Young made elaborate plans to evacuate and, if necessary, destroy the entire city behind them. But what to do about the temple whose massive excavation was already completed and its 8' x 16' foundational walls firmly in place? They did the only thing they could do—they filled it all back in again. Every shovelful. All that soil and gravel that had been so painstakingly removed with those nine thousand days of labor was filled back in. When they finished, those acres looked like nothing more interesting than a field that had been plowed up and left unplanted.

When the Utah War threat had been removed, the Saints returned to their homes and painfully worked again at uncovering the foundation and removing the material from the excavated basement structure.

But then the apparent masochism of all this seemed most evident when not adobes or sandstone but massive granite boulders were selected for the basic construction material. And they were twenty miles away in Little Cottonwood Canyon. Furthermore, the precise design and dimensions of every one of the thousands of stones to be used in that massive structure had to be marked out individually in the architect's office and shaped accordingly. This was a suffocatingly slow process. Just to put *one* layer of the six hundred hand-sketched, individually squared, and precisely cut stones around the building took nearly three years. That progress was so slow that virtually no one walking by the temple block could ever see any progress at all.

And, of course, getting the stone from the mountain to the city center was a nightmare. A canal on which to convey the stone was begun and a great deal of labor and money expended on it, but it was finally aborted. Other means were tried, but oxen proved to be the only viable means of transportation. In the 1860s and '70s always four and often six oxen in a team could be seen almost any working day of the year, toiling and tugging and struggling to pull from the quarry one monstrous block of granite, or at most two of medium size.

During that time, as if the United States Army hadn't been enough, the Saints had plenty of other interruptions. The arrival of the railroad pulled almost all of the working force off the temple for nearly three years, and twice grasshopper invasions sent the workers into full-time summer combat with the pests. By mid-1871, fully two decades and untold misery after it had begun, the walls of the temple were barely visible above ground. Far more visible was the teamster's route from Cottonwood, strewn with the wreckage of wagons—and dreams—unable to bear the load placed on them. The journals and histories of these teamsters are filled with accounts of broken axles, mud-mired animals, shattered sprockets, and shattered hopes. I do not have any evidence that these men swore, but surely they might have been seen turning a rather steely eye toward heaven. But they believed and kept pulling. And through all of this, President Young seemed in no hurry. "The Temple will be built as soon as we are prepared to use it," he said.[5] Indeed his vision was so lofty and his hope so broad that right in the middle of this staggering effort requiring virtually all that the Saints could seem to bear, he announced the construction of the St. George, Manti, and Logan Temples.

"Can you accomplish the work, you Latter-day Saints of these several counties?" he asked. And then in his own inimitable way he answered:

Yes; that is a question I can answer readily. You are perfectly able to do it. The question is, have you the necessary faith? Have you sufficient of the Spirit of God in your hearts to say, yes, by the help of God our Father we will erect these buildings to his name? . . . Go to now, with your might and with your means and finish this Temple.[6]

So they squared their shoulders, stiffened their backs, and went forward with their might. But when President Brigham Young died in 1877, the temple was still scarcely twenty feet above the ground. Ten years later, his successor, President John Taylor, and the temple's original architect, Truman O. Angell, were dead as well. The side walls were just up to the square. And now the infamous Edmunds-Tucker Act had already been passed by Congress disincorporating The Church of Jesus Christ of Latter-day Saints. One of the effects of this law was to put the Church into receivership, whereby the U.S. marshal under a November court order seized this temple the Saints had now spent just under forty years of their lives dreaming of, working for, and praying fervently to enjoy. To all appearances, the still unfinished but increasingly magnificent structure was to be wrested at this last hour from its rightful owners and put into the hands of aliens and enemies, the very group who had often boasted that the Latter-day Saints would never be permitted to finish the building. It seemed those boasts were certain to be fulfilled. Schemes were immediately put forward to divert the intended use of the temple in ways that would desecrate its holy purpose and mock the staggering sacrifice of the Saints who had so faithfully tried to build it.

But God was with these modern children of Israel, as he always has been and always will be. They did all they could do and left the rest in his hands. And the Red Sea parted before them, and they walked through on firm, dry ground. On 6 April 1892, the Saints as a body were nearly delirious. Now, finally, here in their own valley with their own hands they had cut out of the mountains a granite monument that was to mark, after all they had gone through, the safety of the Saints and the permanence of Christ's true church on earth for this one last dispensation. The central symbol of all that was the completed House of their God. The streets were literally jammed with people. Forty thousand of them fought their way onto the temple grounds.

Ten thousand more, unable to gain entrance, scrambled to the tops of nearby buildings in hopes that some glimpse of the activities might be had. Inside the Tabernacle, President Wilford Woodruff, visibly moved by the significance of the moment, said:

> If there is any scene on the face of this earth that will attract the attention of the God of heaven and the heavenly host, it is the one before us today—the assembling of this people, the shout of "Hosanna!" the laying of the topstone of this Temple in honor to our God.[7]

Then, moving outside, he laid the capstone in place exactly at high noon.

In the writing of one who was there, "The scene that followed is beyond the power of language to describe." Lorenzo Snow, beloved President of the Quorum of the Twelve Apostles, came forward leading 40,000 Latter-day Saints in the Hosanna Shout. Every hand held a handkerchief every eye was filled with tears. One said the very "ground seemed to tremble with the volume of the sound" which echoed off the tops of the mountains. "A grander or more imposing spectacle than this ceremony of laying the Temple capstone is not recorded in history."[8] It was finally and forever finished.

Later that year the prestigious *Scientific American* (1892), referred to this majestic new edifice as a "monument to Mormon perseverance." And so it was. Blood, toil, tears, and sweat. The best things are always worth finishing.

Notes

1. Reprint: Previously published in Jeffrey R. Holland, "However Long and Hard the Road" (Brigham Young University devotional, Jan. 18, 1983).
2. James H. Anderson, "The Salt Lake Temple," *Contributor* (The Young Men's Mutual Improvement Associations of Zion), no. 6 (Apr. 1893): 243.
3. Anderson, *Contributor*, 257–58.
4. J. A. Widtsoe, ed., *Discourses of Brigham Young* (Deseret Book, 1973), 410.
5. Anderson, *Contributor*, 266.
6. Anderson, *Contributor*, 267.
7. Anderson, *Contributor*, 270.
8. Anderson, *Contributor*, 273.

James Campbell Livingston: Laying the Foundation of a Great Work

Jeanne W. Anderson[1]

JAMES CAMPBELL LIVINGSTON WAS BORN ON DECEMBER 2, 1833, TO Archibald Livingston and Helen Conner Livingston. He lived with his family at Shotts Iron Works in Lanarkshire, Scotland. Shotts was an industrial town with a large supply of coal, ironstone, and lime in the area. When his parents died of the dreaded cholera, James and his brother Charles worked extensive hours in the coal mine to support the family of six children.

In Scotland, James and his family were blessed to learn the gospel from missionaries from The Church of Jesus Christ of Latter-day Saints. James was baptized and confirmed a member of the Church on May 7, 1849, by Elder Paul Gourley.

In the spring of 1853, when James was nineteen years old, his family decided that he should go on ahead to help pave the way for the others by emigrating to Zion in the Salt Lake Valley. On March 15, 1853, James bid farewell to his family and sailed from Glasgow, Scotland, to Liverpool, England. He then left England on March 28 on the good ship *Falcon*. The company arrived in New Orleans and then transferred to a steamboat to travel up the Mississippi River to Keokuk, Illinois, the staging area for many pioneer companies.

James was assigned to herd and guard the oxen as the wagon trains were organized for the great journey to the Rocky Mountains. He drove an ox team, walking and fording streams the entire distance across the plains from the Mississippi River to the Great Salt Lake, arriving in Salt Lake City on October 16, 1853. James recorded in his journal, "Despite the hardships of the journey, the Lord blessed me by sea and by land, for which I was very thankful, especially for the good health I enjoyed."[2]

Work at the Red Butte Canyon Quarry

Upon his arrival, James was assigned by President Brigham Young to work in the Red Butte Canyon quarry extracting sandstone rock for a wall around the temple block. He worked at the quarry all winter and the following spring and summer.

Prior to James's arrival in Salt Lake City on February 14, 1853, ground had been broken for the Salt Lake Temple, and the cornerstones were laid in a twenty-foot-wide and sixteen-foot-deep perimeter.

James married Agnes Widdison on June 7, 1854. James and Agnes had grown up together as friends in Scotland. They established their first little one-room home in Salt Lake City. After his marriage, James continued to work at the Red Butte quarry extracting the sandstone rock that was used for the fifteen-foot-high wall around the temple block until its completion in May 1857.

Johnston's Army

In June 1857 the first stones were laid on the foundation of the temple; however, the Saints received a message that Johnston's Army was coming to the Utah Territory. This news put a stop to all work on the temple. With the army approaching, Brigham Young instructed the workers to bury the foundation of the temple so that enemies would not desecrate it. Along with thirty thousand other people, the Livingston family left Salt Lake City to temporarily hide out in central Utah.

In anticipation of the army's arrival, Church leaders called up the Mormon Militia, also known as the Nauvoo Legion. James and others were released from working at the quarry and called upon to serve in the militia to hamper Colonel Johnston's approach into the Salt Lake Valley. After further negotiations between the Church and the US Army, Camp Floyd, southwest of Salt Lake City, was established so the army could continue to "monitor" the Utah Territory.

Little Cottonwood Canyon Quarry Work Begins

With the imminent threat eliminated, James was called in 1860 to take a group of forty men and start extracting granite from the mouth of Little Cottonwood Canyon for the Salt Lake Temple. They worked ten-hour days, spring through fall, under the direction of Bishop John Sharp, with James serving as the quarry superintendent. Quarry work paid as follows:

- Master stonemasons and apprentices: $2.00 to $3.00 per day.
- Teamsters: $4.00 to $6.00 per day (they supplied their own wagons and supplies).
- Blacksmiths to sharpen tools and repair wagons: $2.50 to $3.00 per day.

With the start of the Civil War in 1861, Johnston's Army was ordered back to the eastern United States. Shortly thereafter, President Young recommenced temple construction by uncovering the temple foundation. It was discovered that the original sandstone block foundation had cracked, rendering it insufficient to support the granite walls of the new temple. Consequently, the defective blocks were removed and new blocks were placed. The more precisely sized blocks required less mortar, creating a more solid foundation. The new foundation consisted of a sixteen-foot-deep sandstone sub-foundation with a fourteen-foot-deep granite foundation laid over the top.[3]

Coming of the Railroad

The biggest challenge at the Cottonwood Canyon Quarry was transporting the 2,500- to 5,600-pound granite blocks to the temple site.[4] It took four days to transport one large block from the quarry, pulled by wagons with oxen, mules, or horses, to the temple site. Because the wagons often broke down, the Cottonwood Canal was dug to float the granite blocks on barges. This method failed as the soil was too porous to maintain enough water in the canal to support the heavy barges.

During this same period, the Transcontinental Railroad was under construction to connect the country from east to west. President Brigham Young called a stop to the work at the quarry in 1868 and asked the crew to go to work for the railroad. Responding to the quarry workers' confusion, President Young explained that little progress would be made on the temple until the railroad was built. Once the Transcontinental Railroad was completed, other lines could be built, including a line that would extend to the Cottonwood Canyon Quarry.

The 100-worker crew started grading the railbed at Devil's Gate in Weber Canyon. Including completing two tunnels, they finished the work in Weber Canyon in February 1869. James then took a 300-worker crew to Promontory Point in northwest Utah on a heavy rock contract. There the nearby bedrock was broken up with explosives to create gravel ballast under the new rail line.

An Accident

The work was dangerous, and there were tragic accidents of all kinds, mainly because of the volatile and unpredictable explosives. Sometimes heavy explosions started avalanches that buried alive entire camps of workers. It was at Promontory that James was using nitroglycerin when it prematurely exploded, shattering his right arm and hand so badly that his hand had to be amputated one year later.

After James recovered from his accident, he went back to work at the Cottonwood Canyon Quarry. He was fitted with a hook, making the work much more difficult, but he felt blessed to be alive. While the crew continued to transport rock to the temple site by wagons, a railroad extension to the canyon was under construction.

Five years later, on May 3, 1874, the first granite blocks were shipped on railroad flatbed cars. The trip took one hour instead of four days. It was a day of great rejoicing! Sixty-thousand pounds of granite could now be hauled to the temple site in one day. President Brigham Young traveled on the train to personally experience this remarkable event.

The quarry families and the railroad men established the Wasatch settlement in Little Cottonwood Canyon. There they lived in small cabins with wooden floors, wood sides, and tent roofs. These cabins were on the south side of the stream and were reached by a footbridge.

Many leaders of the Church used the area as a summer retreat. The Apostle Wilford Woodruff described the little Wasatch community in this way: "The granite settlement is one of the most romantic spots on the face of the earth for a settlement in the summertime for rest, health, and recreation that I ever beheld. The Little Cottonwood Creek of cold pure ice water rushes down the canyon which abounds with trout and furnishes water for every house and flower bed. It is a delightful and healthy retreat."[5]

Tribute to the Quarry Workers

While the quarry crew relaxed and enjoyed the beauty of the canyon on the Sabbath day, on the other days of the week they engaged in hard, dangerous, and exhausting work. David Cameron, one of the quarry workers, described work at the quarry as follows:

> We learned what it meant to labor for the Lord. It was difficult to get supplies—the men often went hungry! Many times, they were sick with mountain fever or rabbit fever. They suffered from snake bites and bee stings and from mosquitos and horseflies! Imagine, if you can, being blinded by the glistening shafts of sunlight on those white cliffs and deafened by the roaring of all the loosened boulders. Blistering in the blasts, then freezing off fingers and toes! Shuddering during sudden thunderstorms with lightning flashes—being soaked in the rain showers or being pelted with hailstorms and later covered with snow! It seemed as though we were forever climbing, straining, stumbling, falling—fearing for our very lives! But working on to the dead of winter! Then, going home for Christmas to stay a few weeks determined to a man to find other employment. We had to please a lot of people besides John Sharp in charge of the Quarry Mission and Truman O. Angell who drafted till his fingers ached on Brother Young's inspired temple design. Then when we were called into President Young's office to be blessed for our labors, we knew we were not working for Brother Brigham or for anyone else but for the Lord. We labored for His House—not our own; for Him, not for ourselves! We extracted a

Granite Temple from the everlasting hills with our bare hands (so to speak) for all the world to see and enjoy for centuries to come and for the benefit of millions for time and all eternity! Would you do it? Maybe not, but we did do it for the everlasting benefit of all!"[6]

And so the men pressed on in their labors for another fifteen years. On April 6, 1892, the final capstone was laid with 40,000 people in attendance. President Wilford Woodruff pressed an electric button and the temple capstone moved securely into position. The scene that followed is beyond the power of language to describe. The President of the Twelve, Lorenzo Snow, instructed the congregation as to the order of ceremony at the laying of the capstone of the temple. Those gathered on the temple block were to shout "Hosanna" after the stone was placed to indicate that their hearts were "full of thanksgiving to the God of heaven."[7]

The last job at the quarry was to extract rock for the Brigham Young Monument at Temple Square. After the completion of the temple and monument, the rock quarry was closed.

James and his family were called to start a new settlement in Sanpete County at a place called Cedar Cliff. After forty years of hard work, they felt great sorrow in leaving the Salt Lake Temple behind. Fortunately, the Manti Temple had been built, but it was still a full-day wagon journey away. Cedar Cliff was a desolate land of sagebrush and cedar, but it was time to press forward in a new adventure. The family cleared the land and became farmers and ranchers, growing hay and raising cattle.

James was called to serve as the patriarch of the South Sanpete Stake. He died on October 17, 1909, at the age of seventy-five after a lingering illness. He is buried in the cemetery in Fountain Green, Utah.

Notes

1. Note from the author: I am the great-great-granddaughter of James Campbell Livingston and Hannah Widdison Livingston. My source for this article was the *Autobiography of James Campbell Livingston*, which is in my possession.
2. *Autobiography of James Campbell Livingston*, 2.
3. Lynn Arave, "Is the Foundation of the Salt Lake Temple Composed of Granite or Sandstone?," *Deseret News*, May 13, 2018.

4. Modern geologists have determined that the "granite" in Little Cottonwood Canyon used to build the Salt Lake Temple is technically quartz monzonite. However, if the rock had a slightly larger concentration of quartz, it would be considered granite. I chose to use the common term *granite* for this article because that's the term the pioneer builders used.
5. *The Upper Quarries*, comp. Paul A. Hanks, Sept. 26, 1992, MSS in Church Historian's Office, Salt Lake City.
6. *The Upper Quarries*.
7. "Temple Capstone Laid 100 Years Ago," *Deseret News*, Apr. 4, 1992.

John R. Moyle's Long Walk to the Temple

Mark D. Ogletree

"My dear brothers and sisters, may you focus on the temple in ways you never have before. I bless you to grow closer to God and Jesus Christ every day. I love you." —President Russell M. Nelson

YEARS AGO, ELDER JAMES E. FAUST WAS AT THE SALT LAKE CITY airport with Elder Spencer J. Condie. As they were making their way through the terminal, they ran into a devoted and faithful couple whom both men had known for many years. Elder Faust related, "This couple has spent a lifetime of service, meekly, faithfully, and effectively trying to build up the Church in many places in the world." As the two leaders left to make their connecting flight, Elder Condie noted, "Isn't it remarkable what people with five loaves and two fishes do to build up the kingdom of God." Then Elder Faust observed, "This kind of quiet, devoted service to me is surely a fulfillment of the word of God 'that the fulness of [His] gospel might be proclaimed by the weak and the simple unto the ends of the world, and before kings and rulers' (Doctrine and Covenants 1:23)."[1]

One such Latter-day Saint with "five loaves and two fishes" was a stalwart man named John Rowe Moyle. John was born in Cornwall,

England, on February 22, 1808. As a young boy, he worked in the tin mines of Cornwall and then later learned the stonemasonry trade from his father. In 1851, when John was forty-two, he and his family joined The Church of Jesus Christ of Latter-day Saints.[2] In 1856 the Moyles immigrated to America and then joined the Edmund Ellsworth Company—one of the first handcart companies that left Iowa on June 9, arriving in Salt Lake City by September 26, 1856.[3]

After arriving in the Salt Lake Valley, the Moyle family eventually settled in Alpine, Utah—a little over thirty miles south of Salt Lake City. John traveled frequently to Salt Lake City to work on the unfinished Salt Lake Temple. He was a stonemason, and his skills became critical for the masonry work he supervised. John worked at the temple site for over twenty years. President Dieter F. Uchtdorf explained, "Every Monday John left home at two o'clock in the morning and walked six hours in order to be at his post on time. On Friday he would leave his work at five o'clock in the evening and walk almost until midnight before arriving home."[4] If John R. Moyle's twenty years of service were the only thing to mention about him, his story would be remarkable. His walks from Alpine to Salt Lake City and back again for over two decades represent one of the greatest stories of Church service ever told.

However, there is much more to share about John R. Moyle and his devotion to the Lord. One of the most significant experiences in the life of John and his family is when he lost one of his legs in a farming accident. Although there are several versions of this story, the account shared by Elder Vaughn J. Featherstone includes the most detail:

> Not long ago in one of our quorum meetings, Elder W. Eugene Hansen of the Seven Presidents of the Seventy shared a story with us. Elder Theodore M. Burton's great grandfather, John R. Moyle, lived down in Alpine, Utah. That is about twenty-two miles from the Salt Lake Temple if you cut across Corner Canyon. He was the head superintendent of masonry at the temple. He would walk to work at 8:00 a.m. on Monday, and then he would finish at 5:00 p.m. on Friday and walk back home. Then he would leave early enough Sunday night to walk back to work by 8:00 a.m. on

Monday. He did that the whole time he was on his mission as the head masonry superintendent.[5]

One time when he was home on the weekend, he went to milk his cow. Perhaps his hands were cold or the cow was frightened, and the animal kicked him and shattered the bone below the knee of one leg.[6] They didn't have any way to repair it in that day. They simply took a door off the hinges, laid him on the door, and strapped him to it. Then they took the bucksaw they had been using to cut branches from a tree, and they amputated his leg just a few inches below the knee.[7] He should have caught infection, but he didn't. They pulled the flesh down over the bone and sewed it together somehow. When it started to heal, he took a piece of wood and made a peg leg. He carved a little bowl in it and lined the inside of the bowl with a piece of leather. He made straps to fit around his waist and hold the leg in place. When he could get up, he put it on. You can imagine the pain of walking around the house with that wooden leg. After a while he walked around the yard, and then around the fence line of his farm. When he thought he could, he walked twenty-two miles to the Salt Lake Temple, climbed up the scaffolding, and chiseled "Holiness to the Lord" on the wall of temple. I will love him forever for that. I want to meet him someday.[8]

Many have been deeply affected by the faithfulness and commitment of this man—John R. Moyle—who would walk to the Salt Lake Temple each week, for many years, to serve his "mission of masonry." His legacy is one of hard work, sacrifice, and pure dedication. Of course, many have been inspired by Brother Moyle's twenty-two-mile walk to the temple block on his peg leg to chisel "Holiness to the Lord" on the east side of the Salt Lake Temple.

John died on January 15, 1889—almost four years before the Salt Lake Temple would be dedicated.[9] The perseverance, commitment, and fortitude of this stalwart Saint has been so potent that his story has been shared in general conferences by both President Jeffrey R. Holland[10] and President Dieter F. Uchtdorf.[11] Furthermore, it was John R. Moyle's likeness that became the inspiration for the Handcart Pioneer Monument on Temple Square.[12]

In our day, many youth groups have trekked from their Salt Lake County locations to the Salt Lake Temple, trying to capture the spirit of consecration and sacrifice taught to each of us by John R. Moyle. His story depicts love for a cause, devotion, perseverance, faithfulness, and pure consecration. Many years ago, the Presiding Bishop of the Church, Victor L. Brown, taught, "Only if you sacrifice for a cause will you love it."[13] Without a doubt, John R. Moyle made incredible sacrifices to build the kingdom of God on this earth, and consequently, he loved being engaged in the Lord's work. He loved The Church of Jesus Christ of Latter-day Saints with his whole soul.

Years ago, Elder J. Golden Kimball, speaking of the Salt Lake Temple, declared, "When I think about [the temple], every stone is a sermon to me. It tells of suffering, it tells of sacrifice, it preaches—every rock in it, preaches a discourse. . . . Every window, every steeple, everything about the Temple speaks of the things of God, and gives evidence of the faith of the people who built it."[14] The next time you look up at the majestic Salt Lake Temple and you see the stones, the windows, and the spires, think of John R. Moyle and the personal sacrifices he made to build such a sacred edifice.

President Dieter F. Uchtdorf paid a final tribute to John R. Moyle when he stated, "Years later, John's grandson Henry D. Moyle was called as a member of the Quorum of the Twelve and eventually served in the First Presidency of the Church. President Moyle's service in these callings was honorable, but his grandfather John's service is just as pleasing to the Lord. John's legacy of sacrifice serves as a banner of faithfulness."[15]

Notes

1. James E. Faust, in Conference Report, Apr. 1994, 3.
2. "John Rowe Moyle," Wikipedia, accessed Feb. 28, 2024, https://en.wikipedia.org/wiki/John_Rowe_Moyle.
3. "Edmund Ellsworth Company (1856)," Church History Biographical Database, accessed Feb. 28, 2024, https://history.churchofjesuschrist.org/chd/organization/pioneer-company/edmund-ellsworth-company-1856.
4. Dieter F. Uchtdorf, "A Banner of Faithfulness," *Friend*, Feb. 2010, 2.
5. This tragedy occurred when John was in his seventies. See Erica Palmer, "Descendants of Mormon Pioneer John R. Moyle Learn 'They Can Do Hard Things,'" *Deseret News*, Aug. 7, 2014.
6. In the Moyle family history, we learn that "it was a nasty fracture of a compound nature and the bone stuck through the flesh." Gene A. Sessions, ed., *Biographies*

and Reminiscences from the James Henry Moyle Collection, The Archives of the Church of Jesus Christ of Latter-day Saints (n.p., 1974), 202.

7. The Moyle family history adds, "They gave him a big drink of whiskey and a leaden bullet to bite his teeth on, tied him to a door and then with a bucksaw, sawed off his leg, bound the flesh over the stump and allowed it to heal." *James Henry Moyle Collection*, 202–3.
8. Vaughn J. Featherstone, *Man of Holiness* (Deseret Book, 1998), 140–41.
9. "John Rowe Moyle."
10. Jeffrey R. Holland, "As Doves to Our Windows," *Ensign*, May 2000, 75–77.
11. Dieter F. Uchtdorf, "Lift Where You Stand," *Ensign*, Nov. 2008, 53–56.
12. Scott R. Lloyd, "Sculpture Bound for Norway," *Church News*, Feb. 7, 2009.
13. Victor L. Brown, "The Vision of the Aaronic Priesthood," *Ensign*, Nov. 1975, 66.
14. J. Golden Kimball, in Conference Report, Apr. 1915, 79.
15. Dieter F. Uchtdorf, "A Banner of Faithfulness," 2.

The Building of the Salt Lake Temple

Maclane E. Heward

MANY LATTER-DAY SAINTS ARE AWARE OF THE REALITY THAT THE Salt Lake Temple took decades to build. Some may know that it took just over forty years to complete. Still fewer know of the specific challenges faced by the Saints as they undertook such a massive construction project while trying to carve out a sustainable living on the western frontier. Understanding some of the challenges faced during the construction of the Salt Lake Temple can create a sense of awe and gratitude for the sacrifice and commitment of early Latter-day Saints as they dedicated themselves to building a house to their God, a place where God could "manifest himself to [His] people" (Doctrine and Covenants 110:7). Their story can give current Saints strength as we live our story. Difficulty and opposition are not new; the use of agency in overcoming challenges with God's help is part of our spiritual heritage. These truths are manifested in the structure and existence of the Salt Lake Temple.

While the story of the building of the Salt Lake Temple could begin with the First Vision of the Prophet Joseph Smith, we will begin with his vision and views of the land of Zion. Just a few months after the Church was officially organized according to New York state law, Joseph received a revelation directing Oliver Cowdery to lead a mission with three others "unto the Lamanites," declaring that Zion would be built and established "on the borders" of the western frontier (Doctrine and Covenants 28:8–9). In December 1830, and in connection with his translation of the New Testament, Joseph received additional information about Zion that included a view that a people could be prepared to have the Lord "[dwell] in the midst of Zion" (Moses 7:69). At a conference in Kirtland a few months later, the Lord directed Joseph and Oliver to travel to Missouri, where the Lord would make known the location of the "land of [their] inheritance" (Doctrine and Covenants 52:5). Upon arriving in Missouri, Independence was identified as the "center place," and "a spot for the temple" was located (Doctrine and Covenants 57:3).

Over the next thirteen years, Joseph sought to establish Zion as a community and a location with the temple and the presence of God at its center. The Saints were driven from Jackson County and Caldwell County, and they were eventually driven from Nauvoo, Illinois. But in each location, they sought to build a house in which the Lord could manifest Himself to His people. They exemplified for us what it means to be a people of vision, a people who allowed the blessings of God, despite the opposition of humans, to guide their efforts.

Joseph Smith's vision of having a temple at the center of the community was not lost as Brigham Young began to lead the Latter-day Saints first across the Midwest and then to the Rocky Mountains. Entering the Salt Lake Valley on Saturday, July 24, 1847, stricken with what was referred to as mountain fever, Brigham Young had enough strength to identify the valley as the location for the settling of the Saints. The next day, Sunday, Brigham spoke briefly during their worship service to encourage the Saints despite his feeble state of health. On Monday, July 26, still weak, Brigham told Wilford Woodruff that he wanted to take a walk and observe the area. Traveling both by wagon and by foot, Brigham stepped out of Wilford's wagon, walked a short distance, and drove his cane into the ground, declaring, "Here shall stand the temple of our God."[1]

This statement went through Wilford like "lightning," and he asked the company to wait so that he could mark the very spot. He later recalled, "I did nothing else until I put a stake in that spot that he marked with his cane." Wilford remembered the moment and introspectively asked what motivated Brigham to make such a prediction. His remarks came fifty years after that moment in 1847 and four years after the predicted temple was dedicated. He summarized that completing the temple had taken approximately $4 million and 100,000 working men with money in hand. Yet those working with Brigham at the time comprised only 140 men with no money, no permanent dwellings, and no sustainable, established living. Yet the vision remained, and the promises that God gave would be realized through the Saints' determination, efforts, and discipleship.

Because of the immediate needs related to establishing, sustaining, and preparing for the gathering of the Saints, the official groundbreaking for the temple did not take place until February 14, 1853. During the groundbreaking ceremony, Brigham Young drove a spade into the ground and warned, "Get out of my way, for I am going to throw this."[2] Following this act, the crowd rushed to the spot to participate in excavating the foundation, something Brigham wanted completed in just a few months.[3] According to his directions, the dedication of the cornerstones took place not two months later, on April 6, 1853.[4]

Some 6,000 individuals looked on as each of the four cornerstones was dedicated on April 6, 1853. Each cornerstone was dedicated separately following an oration delivered by various leaders. The two eastern cornerstones were dedicated by individuals representing the First Presidency, the Quorum of the Twelve Apostles, the Patriarch to the Church, the Seventies, and the elders. The two stones on the west were dedicated by individuals representing the Aaronic Priesthood: stake presidencies, high priests, and high councils.[5]

The footings, the first layer upon which the foundation wall would rest, were pyramidal in shape. They were wide enough at the top for the eight-to-ten-foot foundation wall to rest upon and tapered outward to distribute the immense weight of the temple to a width of sixteen feet. The primary material for the footings came from the Red Butte Canyon Sandstone quarry. A flagging layer was laid across the footings and was intended to provide a completely level and secure surface from which to build the massive temple structure.[6]

Despite the temple-building project beginning only two years previous, progress slowed in 1855 and then stopped in 1857 due to natural and political factors. Poor harvests, an infestation of crickets, and the continued influx of immigrants forced Brigham to prioritize growing crops and feeding people over building the temple. It was around this same time that the decision was made to use granite from the Cottonwood canyons some sixteen to eighteen miles away. The Utah Territorial Legislative Assembly gave permission for the building of a canal to transport granite blocks to the temple site, and work transitioned to the canal instead of the temple. Because the soil was so porous, the water in the canal seeped into the rocky soil at the mouth of the canyons long before it ever reached Temple Square, and even though much time and effort was dedicated to the project, no granite blocks were ever transported to the temple site in this manner.[7] Thus the Saints moved the initial blocks—which weighed between 2,500 and 5,600 pounds—from the granite quarries to the temple site by oxen and special wagon, which took two to four days or longer if rain hampered their progress.[8]

In building the canal, the Saints relied on their own best guess as to how to transport the granite blocks. It had not worked out as they had planned. If nothing else, they had learned how not to transport the blocks and had gained a source of irrigation for local farming.[9] Even building a house to God, the Saints were not given through revelation all the particulars of the work. In 1831 the Lord had taught a group of Saints that the building of Zion would not be given in a step-by-step process. "It is not meet," explained the Lord, "that I should command in all things. . . . Men should . . . do many things of their own free will" (Doctrine and Covenants 58:26–27). This same reality was also true as the Saints built the temple, and it will continue to be true for Saints in every time and location who seek to build Zion. Despite the setbacks, which were bound to happen, the Saints continued toward the fulfillment of the Lord's vision.

Truman Angell, who had been working on the architectural plans for the temple through January 1856, was exhausted and somewhat depressed. At this point, Brigham sent him on an architectural mission to Europe to "view the various specimens of architecture . . . [where he would] wonder at the works of the ancients, . . . be quick to comprehend the architectural designs of men, take drafts of valuable works, . . . and be better qualified to continue . . . work . . . upon the temple."[10] Angell had learned from the best available earthly knowledge so that he could utilize it for God's purposes, an approach that prophets still support. President Gordon B. Hinckley directed the young people of the Church as follows: "You need all the education you can get. . . . Sacrifice anything that is needed to be sacrificed to qualify yourselves to do the work of the world. . . . You will bring honor to the Church and you will be generously blessed."[11] Despite Angell's absence and the slowing of progress from July 13, 1856, to May 29, 1857, he was learning from the best of the world and would bring honor to the Church and blessings from the Lord as he helped build God's temple.[12]

Less than two months after Angell was reunited with the Saints, on Pioneer Day, July 24, 1857, Brigham received news that a potentially hostile military force of 1,500 men had been sent to Utah by the United States government, with more expected to follow. Why were the troops coming to Utah? They were to put down the rebellion in Utah.[13] The federal government had received exaggerated reports of Latter-day Saint misconduct and overreach, which led President James Buchanan to send the military. The fact that President Buchanan had not informed Brigham Young, the territorial governor, of his plans only exacerbated the situation. Brigham Young and members of the Church, some still carrying the physical marks of persecution and many others possessing the emotional wounds, prepared for the worst, including being driven again from their homes, persecuted, and perhaps even killed.[14] While preparations began immediately, the troops were delayed in their travels, in part through the intentional efforts of the Saints, until the summer of 1858.[15] In hindsight, both the United States government and the Latter-day Saints had overreacted to a powder-keg situation.

The impact of the overreaction extended far beyond the construction of the Salt Lake Temple and included moving the residents of the Salt Lake Valley, nearly 30,000 people, south to Utah Valley and other locations. A few individuals were even assigned to burn down the city if it became apparent that the troops meant to use the fruits of the Saints' labors against them in the ensuing conflict. Regarding the temple, Brigham thought it best that the temple lot look like a plowed field when the military arrived rather than the preparations for a massive structure built of stone. For this reason, Brigham had the stones that were already on the temple lot, but not yet put in place, deposited into the hole that had been dug for the foundation and basement of the temple and then covered with dirt.[16] Though the relationship with the military remained tense, some Saints began moving back into their homes as early as July 1858.[17]

Succinctly put, the Latter-day Saints' reaction in Salt Lake in 1858 was directly connected to the persecutions they had previously experienced in the East in the early 1830s. These persecutions, particularly in Missouri, left many Saints equating the military with a mob. During the Missouri conflict, it was difficult if not impossible to distinguish those acting as members of official military groups from those acting extralegally. Even military leaders and law enforcement officers, not to mention religious leaders, engaged in threats, hostility, and "war-like" behavior.[18] With these memories still a part of the Saints' experiences, it is understandable why their reaction was dramatic and emotional when in 1858 they heard of the troops coming to Utah to put down the rebellion and remove Brigham Young from his position as territorial governor. Despite the desperate and fear-filled experience, most, though not all, of the Saints maintained their character as peaceful, well-behaved Christians. In moments of difficulty, perhaps even threat, the example of the early Saints reminds us to constantly strive to live as Christ would have us live.[19]

While peaceful negotiations helped to reduce the perception of immediate threat, the temple foundation still was not unearthed until the building season of 1859. By the end of that year, enough dirt had been removed for the architect, Truman Angell, to know that some of the foundation was out of level. How could this have happened with so little weight resting on top of the foundation? The next building season, 1860, brought additional excavation and transportation of granite from the Cottonwood Canyon quarries, but no stone was placed. The lack of progress may have been in part due to uncertainty about how to proceed after the discovery of the settling foundation.

Eventually, portions of the footings were removed to remedy issues seemingly caused by builders taking small shortcuts in the building process, possibly due to a lack of resources.[20] Brigham Young later reflected on the situation by saying, "I took up the rocks. . . . What did I find there[?] Pieces of planks rollers to wedge up those rocks[.] I knew how it looked, and I would not build a house and say I dedicate it to God."[21] Brigham was referring to the fact that large stones were originally put into place with wooden rollers and that some of those rollers were left as part of the footings.

At a different time, Wilford Woodruff recorded in his journal that "President Young said I expect this Temple will stand through the Millennium & the Brethren will go in and give the Endowments to the people and this is the reason why I am having the foundation of the Temple taken up."[22] The desire for the temple to last through the Millennium, and the desire to build a temple to God, motivated the workers to get the job done right. President Thomas S. Monson similarly cautioned against cutting corners as he directed Church members to "choose the harder right instead of the easier wrong."[23] As the Saints in the 1850s demonstrated, sacrificing quality for speed or convenience may provide short-term gains but may lead to long-term setbacks. When participating in the work of the Lord, we ought to work as if our labors will last "for years, and this shall turn unto [us] for [our] good" (Doctrine and Covenants 51:17).

As the footings and foundation walls were strengthened and shored up, an additional layer of stone was added, the flagging course, and by 1865 the temple walls were finally back to the level they had been prior to their burial in 1858. Because this process had taken so long, an excess of stone had been transported to the temple site, and by the end of the 1866 season, between four and six courses of stone, with approximately 600 stones per course, had been laid in place, bringing the construction to ground level.[24]

Work on the temple continued for more than a quarter century, with progress slowing or accelerating in response to various circumstances. During the 1868 building season, labor slowed because of the approaching Transcontinental Railroad, which used both materials and labor previously dedicated to the temple construction. With a railway track running to the temple block from the city station and other connecting lines to the Cottonwood canyons completed in 1873, the railroad that had initially slowed progress now accelerated it.[25] A derrick, a type of crane, was built on-site in 1873, and by 1876 a steam engine had been attached to it. A reemphasis on the united order and the building of the temple in 1876 again accelerated the work; still, approximately a year later, when Brigham died, the walls were only twenty feet high.[26] Over the next two years, an additional twenty-five feet were added to the walls, extending them to forty-five total feet.[27]

By 1885 the temple walls, except for the towers, had been completed, yet building had slowed during the 1880s as a result of the federal raid in which federal officials entered homes and businesses to arrest leaders and Church members practicing plural marriage. This was a time of bitter persecution for the Church that led, for a time, to the confiscation of Temple Square. The enemies of the Church boasted that the Church would never be allowed to finish the temple but that the "Gentiles" would finish it for their own purposes.[28] John Taylor passed away in hiding in July 1887, and Truman Angell, the Church architect, passed away in October 1887. Wilford Woodruff was sustained as the President of the Church in April 1889 and issued the manifesto ending plural marriage eighteen months later.

The temple, in practice and in doctrine, was more important than the continuance of the practice of plural marriage.[29] This act calmed the tensions between the Church and the government, which facilitated accelerated efforts on the temple construction. Artistic missionaries were called in the summer of 1890 and sent to France for training so they could paint murals on the interior temple walls when the time came.[30] The capstone ceremony took place on April 6, 1892, at which Francis M. Lyman, a member of the Quorum of the Twelve Apostles, proposed that all present "pledge themselves collectively and individually, to furnish, as fast as it may be needed, all the money that may be required to complete the temple at the earliest time possible, so that the dedication may take place on April 6th, 1893."[31]

An annex designed by Joseph Don Carlos Young, the Church architect appointed after the death of Truman Angell in 1887, stood approximately 100 feet from the temple proper and was a place for patrons to show their temple recommends and receive names of persons for whom ordinances would be performed. Work on the annex began in 1982 and was completed in time to be dedicated with the temple.[32] Seventy years later this annex was razed when the Church built additional facilities north of the existing temple, which were dedicated in 1967.[33]

The temple was completed, and with time to spare, at noon on April 5, 1893. The public was welcomed inside for an open house that evening from 3 p.m. to 5 p.m., which was attended by approximately 600 community leaders, federal officials, business leaders, and friends of other faiths.[34] During the dedication the next day, there was a terrible storm. Reflecting on the day a century later, President Gordon B. Hinckley said, "A terrible storm arose that day. Rain fell in torrents, and the wind blew with savage fury. It was as if the forces of evil were lashing out in violent protest against this act of consecration." He then said that "all was peace and quiet within the thick granite walls."[35] During this storm, President Wilford Woodruff, in the dedicatory prayer, blessed the buildings on Temple Square and the temple itself to be preserved "from injury or destruction by flood or fire; from the rage of the elements, the shafts of the vivid lightning, the overwhelming blasts of the hurricane, the flames of consuming fire, and the upheavals of the earth-quake, O Lord, protect them."[36]

The Saints had qualified for this blessing through forty years of dedicated work. With the help of the Lord, they had built a structure impervious to the outside storm. In similar fashion, Helaman had taught his sons that if they would build their foundation "upon the rock of our Redeemer, who is Christ, the Son of God . . . that when the devil shall send forth his mighty winds, yea, his shafts in the whirlwind, yea, when all his hail and his mighty storm shall beat upon you, it shall have no power over you to drag you down to the gulf of misery and endless wo, because of the rock upon which ye are built, which is a sure foundation, a foundation whereon if men build they cannot fall" (Helaman 5:12).

Brigham Young wanted the temple to "stand as a proud monument of the faith, perseverance and industry of the Saints of God in the mountains, in the nineteenth century."[37] Surely it does. It also stands as a monument that the faith of Latter-day Saints can lead to the accomplishment of remarkable tasks even through extreme difficulties. The Salt Lake Temple can remind us of the determination to think creatively and work consistently to accomplish the vision God has placed upon us. It reminds us that although we may not always initially know how to accomplish His purposes, that does not mean that setbacks are failures but that setbacks are merely one additional step toward divine success.[38] It can further remind us that we ought to learn all we can from the experts of the world but dedicate our learning to the purposes of God. We can learn that when doing the work of the Lord, we ought to maintain high standards and remember that we are seeking long-term gains.

Each temple built, explained President Hinckley, stands as a latter-day testimony "that God the eternal Father lives, that He has a plan for the blessing of His sons and daughters of all generations, . . . that His Beloved Son . . . is the Savior and Redeemer of the world, whose atoning sacrifice makes possible the fulfillment of that plan in the eternal life of each who accepts and lives the gospel, . . . [and] that life beyond the grave is as real and certain as is mortality."[39] This is particularly true of the Salt Lake Temple because of the dedication and sacrifice of the early Saints in building it—and building it to last.[40]

Fifty-seven years after Joseph Smith dedicated the Kirtland Temple "that the Son of Man might have a place to manifest himself to his people" (Doctrine and Covenants 109:5), Wilford Woodruff dedicated the Salt Lake Temple with the same hope. He pleaded, "That thy glory may rest upon it; that Thy holy presence may be continually in it; that it may be the abode of Thy Well-Beloved Son, our Savior; that the angels who stand before Thy face may be the hallowed messengers who shall visit it, bearing to us Thy wishes and Thy will, that it may be sanctified and consecrated in all its parts holy unto Thee, the God of Israel, the Almighty Ruler of Mankind."[41]

Notes

1. Wilford Woodruff, *Collected Discourses Delivered by Wilford Woodruff, His Two Counselors, The Twelve Apostles, and Others (1896–1898)*, ed. Brian H. Stuy, vol. 5 (B. H. S., 1992), 314–15. See also "July 26, 1847," *Wilford Woodruff Journal, 1847 January–1853 December*, Church History Catalog, 85; "July 26," *William Clayton Diaries*, vol. 2 (1847), 215; and William G. Hartley, A. Gary Anderson, and LaMar C. Berrett, *Sacred Places: A Comprehensive Guide to Early LDS History Sites, Vol. 6 Wyoming and Utah* (Deseret Book, 2006), 66. See also *Saints: No Unhallowed Hand* (Church of Jesus Christ of Latter-day Saints, 2020), 66.

2. John D. T. McAllister journal, Feb. 14, 1853, Church History Library, Salt Lake City. As cited in Jacob W. Olmstead, Josh Probert, and Elwin C. Robison, "Myths and Realities of the Salt Lake Temple Foundation," *Journal of Mormon History* 48, no. 4 (2022): 32–65, https://doi.org/10.5406/24736031.48.4.02.
3. For information about the crowd rushing to participate in the excavation, see Scott Kenney, ed., *Wilford Woodruff's Journals, 1833–1898*, 9 vols. (Signature Books, 1983–1985), 4:198, Feb. 14, 1853 (as cited by Olmstead et al., "Salt Lake Temple Foundation," under the heading "Groundbreaking").
4. Olmstead et al., "Salt Lake Temple Foundation." "Young's confident declaration at the groundbreaking on February 14, 1853, that the cornerstone-laying ceremony for the temple would take place in less than two months on April 6, 1853, put a squeeze on the work."
5. Richard O. Cowan, "The Design, Construction, and Role of the Salt Lake Temple," in *Salt Lake City: The Place Which God Prepared*, ed. Scott C. Esplin and Kenneth L. Alford (Religious Studies Center and Deseret Book, 2011), 49.
6. Olmstead et al., "Salt Lake Temple Foundation."
7. Olmstead et al., "Salt Lake Temple Foundation." See also Ronald W. Walker, Richard E. Turley Jr., and Glen M. Leonard, *Massacre at Mountain Meadows: An American Tragedy* (Oxford University Press, 2008), 91.
8. Richard Neitzel Holzapfel, *Every Stone a Sermon* (Bookcraft, 1992), 22. Olmstead indicates that on a firm roadbed, the journey could be completed in two days. Olmstead et al., "Salt Lake Temple Foundation."
9. David A. Bednar, "An Evening with Elder David A. Bednar" (evening with a General Authority, Feb. 7, 2020). See also Matthew Holland, "Wrong Roads and Revelation," *New Era*, July 2005.
10. Truman O. Angell journal 1857, 8 April 1867–1868, September 24, 1867, MSS, Library Archives, Historical Department, The Church of Jesus Christ of Latter-day Saints, Salt Lake City; hereafter cited as LDS Church Archives. As cited in Paul L. Anderson, "'Truman O. Angell': Architect and Saint," in *Supporting Saints: Life Stories of Nineteenth-Century Mormons* (BYU Religious Studies Center, 1985), 133–73. See also Holzapfel, *Every Stone a Sermon*, 17.
11. Gordon B. Hinckley, "A Prophet's Counsel and Prayer for Youth," *Ensign*, Jan. 2001, 7.
12. Holzapfel, *Every Stone a Sermon*, 17.
13. Juanita Brooks, *The Mountain Meadows Massacre* (University of Oklahoma Press, 1974), 16–18.
14. Much has been said on this topic from a variety of perspectives. Juanita Brooks discusses the tension as the backdrop of the Mountain Meadows Massacre, the focus of her book bearing the same title. In a similar vein, Ronald W. Walker, Richard E. Turley, and Glen M. Leonard undertake the same pursuit in their book *Massacre at Mountain Meadows*. Richard Turley published a condensed overview of the Utah War in an *Ensign* article. Richard E. Turley, "The Mountain Meadows Massacre," *Ensign*, Sept. 2007, 14–17.
15. Olmstead et al., "Salt Lake Temple Foundation."

16. Olmstead et al., "Salt Lake Temple Foundation," 53, n69. See also Holzapfel, *Every Stone a Sermon*, 20. Holzapfel indicated that the stones were hidden to obscure the Saints' efforts.
17. This meant that some Saints could have left their homes in May 1858 and been back in July 1858. Holzapfel, *Every Stone a Sermon*, 20.
18. John Taylor expressed his surprise at his first experience with a mob, saying, "This was the first mob I had ever seen, and the whole affair was new to me, especially when I considered the kind of officers [the mob] had." Referencing the Protestant ministers among the group, Taylor remarked, "I had heretofore looked upon gospel ministers as messengers of peace; here they came not only in a war-like capacity, but as the leaders of an armed mob—a gang of marauders and free-booters, with the avowed object of driving peaceful citizens—men, women and children, from their homes." Even after General Atchison, a general in the Missouri State militia, disbanded and disbursed men in Daviess County, sending both Latter-day Saint defenders and Missouri persecutors home, some Missourians under military leadership stayed in the vicinity and prepared to assault the Saints. B. H. Roberts, *The Life of John Taylor, Third President of The Church of Jesus Christ of Latter-day Saints* (Bookcraft, 1963), 56–57. As quoted in Alexander Baugh, "A Call to Arms: The 1838 Mormon Defense of Northern Missouri" (PhD diss., Brigham Young University, 1996), 153–54. See Baugh, "Call to Arms," 155. Baugh's dissertation offers ample evidence for the mixture of military forces and organizations forming significant elements of the persecutions of the Latter-day Saints.
19. The Mountain Meadow Massacre was one example of a very small group of Saints who temporarily forgot their commitment to act as the Savior in all that they did. Most during this time, however, continued to act in congruity with their Christian morals of peace. See *Saints: No Unhallowed Hand*, 257–69, 272–75.
20. Olmstead et al., "Salt Lake Temple Foundation."
21. Brigham Young, Sermon, April 27, 1868, Pitman Shorthand Transcriptions, as cited in Olmstead et al., "Salt Lake Temple Foundation."
22. Kenney, *Wilford Woodruff's Journals*, 6:71. See also "Remarks by President Brigham Young," *Deseret News*, Oct. 14, 1893, 97. Also found in Brigham Young, *Journal of Discourses*, 10:254.
23. Thomas S. Monson, "Choices," *Ensign* or *Liahona*, May 2016, 86.
24. Olmstead et al., "Salt Lake Temple Foundation."
25. Cowan, "Salt Lake Temple," 51–52. Holzapfel, *Every Stone a Sermon*, 27.
26. Cowan, "Salt Lake Temple," 52.
27. Holzapfel, *Every Stone a Sermon*, 29.
28. Cowan, "Salt Lake Temple," 53.
29. Richard E. Bennett, "Which Is the Wisest Course?: The Transformation in Mormon Temple Consciousness, 1870–1898," *BYU Studies Quarterly* 52 (2013), https://scholarsarchive.byu.edu/byusq/vol52/iss2/2.
30. Holzapfel, *Every Stone a Sermon*, 35–36.
31. *Deseret Evening News*, Apr. 6, 1892, cited in Holzapfel, *Every Stone a Sermon*, 42, 47. Cowan, "Salt Lake Temple," 60, n38.

32. It was built from cream-colored oolite stone quarried in the Manti quarry and was Moorish or Byzantine in appearance, which set it apart from the original structure. Construction began on this annex in 1892, and it was completed in time for it to be dedicated with the rest of the temple structure. Cowan, "Salt Lake Temple," 61–62.
33. This structure included a 400-seat chapel, a subterranean dressing room, a temple ceremony waiting room, and additional sealing rooms. It was dedicated on October 22, 1967, by Hugh B. Brown. Cowan, "Salt Lake Temple," 61–62.
34. Cowan, "Salt Lake Temple," 60.
35. Gordon B. Hinckley, "This Peaceful House of God," *Ensign*, May 1993, 75.
36. "Dedicatory Prayer: Salt Lake Temple, 6 April 1893," The Church of Jesus Christ of Latter-day Saints, accessed May 6, 2024, https://www.churchofjesuschrist.org/temples/details/salt-lake-temple/prayer/1893-04-06.
37. "Remarks by President Brigham Young," *Deseret News*, Oct. 14, 1893, 97.
38. David A. Bednar, "An Evening with Elder David A. Bednar."
39. Gordon B. Hinckley, "This Peaceful House of God."
40. During the original building process, from 1853 to 1893, five workers died as a result of accidents. See Holzapfel, *Every Stone a Sermon*, ix, for names of the deceased.
41. "Dedicatory Prayer: Salt Lake Temple."

"The Temple and Your Spiritual Foundation"

President Russell M. Nelson[1]

AS YOU KNOW, WE ARE PERFORMING MAJOR RENOVATIONS ON THE historic Salt Lake Temple. This complex project includes major reinforcement of its original foundation, which has served well for more than a century. But this temple must stand much longer. In late May, I inspected the progress on this massive project. I thought you would appreciate seeing what my wife Wendy and I saw. I think you'll see why the hymn "How Firm a Foundation" has come to have new meaning for us.

We are looking at the original foundation of the Salt Lake Temple. I am standing in an area beneath what was the Garden Room. As I examine the craftsmanship of this entire building, I marvel at what the pioneers accomplished. I am totally in awe when I consider that they built this magnificent temple with only tools and techniques available to them more than a century ago.

These many decades later, however, if we examine the foundation closely, we can see the effects of erosion, gaps in the original stonework, and varying stages of stability in the masonry.

Now as I witness what modern engineers, architects, and construction experts can do to reinforce that original foundation, I am absolutely amazed. Their work is astonishing!

The foundation of any building, particularly one as large as this one, must be strong and resilient enough to withstand earthquakes, corrosion, high winds, and the inevitable settling that affects all buildings. The complex task of strengthening now underway will reinforce this sacred temple with the foundation that can and will stand the test of time.

We are sparing no effort to give this venerable temple, which had become increasingly *vulnerable*, a foundation that will withstand the forces of nature into the Millennium. . . .

My dear brothers and sisters, when renovations on the Salt Lake Temple are completed, there will be *no safer* place during an earthquake in the Salt Lake Valley than inside that temple.

Notes

1. Reprint: Previously published in Russell M. Nelson, "The Temple and Your Spiritual Foundation," *Liahona*, Nov. 2021, 93–96.

PART 2

PRINCIPLES AND DOCTRINES OF THE TEMPLE

The Holy of Holies and the Salt Lake Temple

Alonzo L. Gaskill & Seth G. Soha

THE TERM *HOLY OF HOLIES* DOESN'T APPEAR ANYWHERE IN THE King James Version (KJV) of the Bible.[1] The KJV sometimes uses the phrase *most holy place* in reference to the Mosaic tabernacle or to the biblical temple, though the words *temple* and *Holy of Holies* are not synonyms.[2] The actual Hebrew term rendered "most holy place" or "sanctuary" (in the KJV) means "apartness" or "separateness," whereas the Hebrew term for "Holy of Holies" is likely derived from a root word that means "to speak."[3] This terminology implies that the ancient Holy of Holies was where the Lord's prophet went to talk with God and where God would "speak" to His prophet. Thus, Elder Bruce R. McConkie explained, "In a general sense, *any* sacred place where oracles [or revelations] are received is called an oracle [or 'place of revelation']. A temple is an oracle in this sense, with *the holy of holies* therein being specifically so designated. (1 Kings 6:16; 8:6; 2 Chron. 4:20; Ps. 28:2.) Sacred revelations or oracles given in such places warrant designating the place itself as an oracle, that is, as a house where revelation is received (Doctrine and Covenants 124:39)."[4]

Sacred texts indicate that the Mosaic tabernacle had its Holy of Holies (Hebrews 9:8–10),[5] as did each of the biblical temples associated with covenant Israel: Solomon's temple (2 Chronicles 3:8),[6] the future temple Ezekiel saw in vision (Ezekiel 40:44–47), Zerubbabel's temple (3 Maccabees 1:6–2:22), and Herod's temple (Matthew 27:51).[7] In addition, just as each Holy of Holies served as a place of communion between God and His chosen servants, so too did the Garden of Eden and certain mountain tops (like Mount Sinai) serve as a "Holy of Holies"—in the Hebrew sense of the word.[8]

Restoration Holy of Holies

While not officially containing a Holy of Holies, Palmyra's Sacred Grove and the Kirtland Temple both functioned in a way similar to the ancient biblical Holy of Holies.[9] Joseph Smith entered both of these locations in an effort to commune with God, and in both places the Prophet heard God "speak" (as the Hebrew term implies that he would). One source conjectured, "It appears that designating a room of the temple as a Holy of Holies began with the earliest temples built by the modern Church. While the Kirtland Temple did not have a specific room set aside as a Holy of Holies . . . [,] because Christ and ancient prophets appeared there, the second-floor east pulpits could be considered the Holy of Holies for that temple."[10]

While the Sacred Grove and Kirtland Temple can be said to have had only quasi–Holy of Holies, less conjectural is the fact that one of the sealing rooms (adjacent to the celestial room) in the original Nauvoo Temple was designated as a Holy of Holies. In it, eternal marriages were performed but so were certain higher ordinances (often referred to in the early Church as the "second endowment" or "second anointing").[11] Evidencing this room's uniqueness (in comparison to other parts of the temple), President Heber C. Kimball expressed concern that some patrons were coming in and out of the Nauvoo Temple "Holy of Holies" and that "this should not be." After the death of Joseph Smith, the "order [was] that no person come into [that sacred] room unless he be invited . . . by the Twelve [Apostles]."[12]

The Manti Utah Temple was originally built with a set-apart room specifically used as a Holy of Holies (in the biblical sense of the word).[13] It is commonly pointed out that after the Church established itself in Utah, the Manti Temple was the site of its only functioning Holy of Holies. Once the Salt Lake Temple was dedicated in 1893,

Manti's Holy of Holies was decommissioned as the place set apart for the Prophet to commune with God and began to be used as a traditional sealing room. Then, in the late 1970s, it was no longer used for sealings either, and its doors were left open (though roped off) so that visitors to the temple could peer into the once-functioning Holy of Holies.[14] Currently, it is again being used for sealing purposes.[15]

On August 18, 1949, President George F. Richards (then serving as President of the Quorum of the Twelve Apostles) wrote a letter to members of the First Presidency and the Council of the Twelve, stating, among other things, "Temples under construction now and in the future should be provided with a room for the administration of these blessings alone,[16] to be known as the Holy of Holies, . . . and temples should be designed and constructed with that thought in mind."[17] President Richards's recommendation was adopted, and certain sealing rooms were designated in each of the temples as "Holy of Holies" in which this higher ordinance was administered. The practice of calling those sealing rooms "Holy of Holies" continued at least until the mid-1960s, as President Richards's son (LeGrand, also a member of the Quorum of the Twelve) used that terminology in a 1966 letter when he referred to the use of temple sealing rooms for performing the ordinance of the Second Anointing.[18] While the Church has continued to use certain sealing rooms in various temples for that same purpose, at some point they moved away from referring to them as "Holy of Holies."[19] As a consequence of the past practice of calling certain sealing rooms "Holy of Holies," there is a common tendency for members to conflate the use of traditional sealing rooms for certain higher ordinances with the Holy of Holies that has been set aside in certain temples (ancient and modern) for the President of the Church to commune with God.[20] Nonetheless, the two rooms appear to have different overarching purposes.

In the traditional sense of the term, the Salt Lake Temple is the only temple of The Church of Jesus Christ of Latter-day Saints that currently has a functioning Holy of Holies—meaning a room dedicated and set apart for God's prophet to commune with Him, and where God would "speak" or "reveal" to His prophet. Thus, Elder Bruce R. McConkie explained, "Temples, now and during the millennium, are to prepare men for a celestial inheritance. When that glorious goal is gained, heaven itself becomes a temple. The holy of holies in the Lord's earthly houses are symbols and types of the Eternal Holy of Holies which is the highest heaven of the celestial world."[21] Just as each of us who achieve celestial glory will commune with God face-to-face, the purpose of a set-apart earthly Holy of Holies is for God's prophet to enter therein, symbolically "part the veil," and commune with the Divine on behalf of God's Church and His children throughout the world.

Design of the Holy of Holies

Three surviving firsthand accounts describe in detail the interior of the Salt Lake Temple's Holy of Holies. The first dates from 1893 and was penned by Eugene Young, a non–Latter-day Saint grandson of President Brigham Young who toured the temple the night before its dedication.[22] The second dates to 1904 and was published by the Bureau of Information and Church Literature, directed to nonmember visitors to the city. The final account was published in 1912 and was written by Elder James E. Talmage for his book *The House of the Lord*.[23] Though Talmage's description was written approximately twenty years after Young's, the two accounts offer very similar details, suggesting that little about the Holy of Holies had changed in those two decades, even though a renovation had been performed on the interior of the Salt Lake Temple in the summer of 1911.[24]

Based on those three descriptions, the following features were true of the temple's Holy of Holies—presumably at least until its significant renovation in the early 1960s, if not to this day. The Holy of Holies was incorporated into what has sometimes been called the "intermediate floor" of the temple, located between the endowment "instruction rooms" and the large "assembly room" (which comprises the temple's upper story).[25] Along the south wall of the celestial room are three sets of sliding doors that are positioned side by side. The center door leads to the Holy of Holies, and the other two lead to traditional sealing rooms.[26] There are two steps in front of each of the three rooms leading up to their doors, elevating them slightly above the floor of the celestial room to which they are attached. However, beyond the external sliding doors of the Holy of Holies are six additional steps that lead up to a second set of doors.[27] These second doors "mark the threshold of the inner room or Holy of Holies of the Temple, and correspond to the inner curtain or veil that shielded from public view the most sacred precincts of [the] Tabernacle and Temple in the earlier dispensations."[28]

Between the exterior doors and the set of doors that opens into the actual Holy of Holies is an "elegant" hand-carved railing (on either side of the stairs).[29] The poles of the rails are in the traditional shape of balustrades—usually equated with the shape of a wild pomegranate flower. These railings lead up to a set of newel posts at the top of the six stairs.[30] The two newel posts originally had bronze cherubic figures attached, which Elder Talmage described as "symbolical of innocent childhood."[31] In addition to the bronze figurines, lights in the form of "flower clusters" illuminated that portion of the entrance to the Holy of Holies. When the temple was first constructed, the "entrance doorway" to the Holy of Holies was "framed in red velvet with an outer border finished in gold."[32] The room itself is circular in shape and fairly small—only eighteen feet in diameter.[33]

Attached to the Holy of Holies—and accessible only through that sacred room[34]—is what has been called an "accouchement room," in which items (needed for "certain higher ordinances") are stored.[35] The ceiling of the Holy of Holies is domed,[36] with significant gold leafing,[37] and features a "set [of] large circles of colored lenses, through which strong incandescent lights throw varied beams of color."[38] Elsewhere we are told that these "colored lenses" are "circular and semicircular" and are made of "jeweled glass" through which "light penetrates into the room in countless hues of subdued intensity."[39] In addition to the unique light that filters through the jeweled glass of the dome, hanging from the ceiling (in the center of the room) is an elaborate vintage chandelier. Also, a series of wall sconces offer supplementary light to the room. The original floor was made of "native hard-wood," consisting of inlaid one-inch "blocks" laid out in "a pattern of great beauty."[40] One observer described the appearance of the floor as having "a pattern" that "gives the appearance of ascending" toward a stained-glass depiction of the Father and Son.[41] In the early twentieth century, a large area rug covered much of the original floor. Later, wall-to-wall carpeting was installed in the entire room.[42] The room's curved walls have four niches, originally bordered in crimson and gold, with painted blue backgrounds. In these niches were once placed vases.[43] Each of the niches is separated by carved pillars that support the series of arches that make up the curved walls of the Holy of Holies.[44] On the room's south side, directly opposite the door that leads into the Holy of Holies, is a twelve-foot stained-glass window that depicts the First Vision,[45] crafted by Tiffany Glass and Decorating Company.[46] Beneath the depiction of the Father and Son appearing to the young Prophet is the inscription "If any of you lack wisdom, let him ask of God, that giveth to all men liberally, and upbraideth not; and it shall be given him" (James 1:5). Just beneath that appears the words "This is my beloved Son, hear Him."[47] In the center of the room, facing the stained-glass depiction, is an ornate altar at which the visiting prophet may kneel and offer up the petitions of his heart.[48]

On December 29, 2019, the Salt Lake Temple was closed to perform a major seismic upgrade to the building but also to complete a significant revamp of the temple's interior, including its floor plan. While we cannot say with certitude, one would assume that the major remodel of the temple's celestial room may very well include an update of the interior of the Holy of Holies. Thus, the description provided herein is representative of how this most sacred of chambers in the Salt Lake Temple originally looked, but it says nothing about how it may appear when the temple is rededicated in 2026.

Salt Lake Temple Holy of Holies

On many levels, the Salt Lake Temple is the Church's "flagship" temple. It is unique in its history, design, and function in The Church of Jesus Christ of Latter-day Saints. It was the first temple on which construction was started once the Saints arrived in the Utah Territory, though not the first to be completed.[49] Ground was broken for the iconic temple on Valentine's Day of 1853. However, it was not dedicated until April 1893, over forty years later. Thus, it was the fourth of the Utah temples to actually be dedicated, after the St. George, Logan, and Manti temples.[50] The reason for this curious fact is found in the Salt Lake Temple's unique design and construction materials.

One source suggested, "The combined presence of the [Salt Lake] Temple and the established headquarters of the Church (with a prophet at its head who professes continued communication with God) appear to satisfy Isaiah's prophecy."[51] The prophecy to which our source refers is found in the second chapter of Isaiah:

> And it shall come to pass in the last days, [that] the mountain of the Lord's house shall be established in the top of the mountains, and shall be exalted above the hills; and all nations shall flow unto it. And many people shall go and say, Come ye, and let us go up to the mountain of the Lord, to the house of the God of Jacob; and he will teach us of his ways, and we will walk in his paths: for out of Zion shall go forth the law, and the word of the Lord from Jerusalem. (Isaiah 2:2–3)

The source continued, "In reference to Isaiah, the Temple has become more than the physical symbol of the Church, it has become the 'spiritual ensign to the world.'"[52] And so it is. In the post–Joseph Smith era of Church history, the Salt Lake Temple may have been the site of more revelations for the entire Church and the whole world than any other edifice on the face of the planet.

In conjunction with fulfilling Isaiah's prophetic vision, and aside from the fact that it took longer to build than any of the other temples of the Restoration, the Salt Lake Temple is also unique in its purpose. One monograph on that sacred edifice noted, "The Salt Lake Temple was designed to serve two functions. Like all temples, it accommodated the needs of the temple ritual: but unlike the others, it was conceived as a place of council where the General Authorities could meet and decide on the doctrinal and administrative matters affecting the Church."[53] This same source goes on to point out that the "third floor [of the Salt Lake Temple] comprises the area of the council chambers. . . . The presence of the Holy of Holies and the administrative function of the third floor makes the Salt Lake Temple unique among temples and other ecclesiastical buildings of the Church" today.[54] Indeed, those "council chambers," along with the Holy of Holies, make the Salt Lake Temple the Church's *only* currently operating temple that is not just a place of salvific work for the living and the dead but also a place where prophets and apostles of this dispensation gather to commune with God, receive revelation for the world, and work to know the mind and will of God for the future of His Church and kingdom upon the earth. No other temple of The Church of Jesus

Christ has this same collection of set-apart spaces reserved for the specific purpose of prophets, seers, and revelators receiving revelation (Mosiah 8:16; Doctrine and Covenants 107:92; 124:94, 125).

In addition to being used (at times) for "the higher ordinances in the Priesthood relating to the exaltation of both living and dead"[55]—the Salt Lake Temple's Holy of Holies is where "the President of the Church may retire when burdened down with heavy decisions to seek an interview with Him whose Church it is. The prophet holds the keys, the spiritual keys and the very literal key to this one door in that sacred edifice."[56] Indeed, the "presiding high priest, the President of the Church, controls access to this sanctuary."[57] Thus, he, and *he alone*, governs who enters and uses this most holy space upon the face of the earth.[58]

Every prophet of this dispensation has received revelations—some well-known and others more closely guarded, some experienced in the temple and others in locations the Lord has hallowed by His presence. For example, when seeking to know the Lord's will regarding the extension of the priesthood to "all worthy male members of the Church," President Spencer W. Kimball spent "many hours alone in prayer and meditation in the Holy of Holies, often after hours when the temple was still" and no one was present. Likewise, when wishing to know what he should do when he learned of the passing of President Wilford Woodruff, President Lorenzo Snow immediately retired to the Holy of Holies (in the Salt Lake Temple) and, dressed in the "robes of the holy priesthood," knelt at the altar and "poured out his heart to the Lord."

While many manifestations have been received by prophets and Presidents of the Church in the Salt Lake Temple—more than can be discussed herein—we will briefly elaborate on Presidents Kimball's and President Snow's revelations on priesthood and succession (respectively), both of which took place in the parts of the Salt Lake Temple largely reserved for members of the First Presidency and the Quorum of the Twelve Apostles.

Regarding President Kimball's pleading with the Lord (in the Holy of Holies) for knowledge regarding the priesthood, and the revelation that came in response, note the words of a few of those present.[59] Elder LeGrand Richards (of the Twelve) described feeling a sudden and "warm, spiritual flush over his entire body. His heart began to beat faster. He was aware that there was an angel in the room and recognized the late prophet Wilford Woodruff sitting among them! . . . The appearance of President Woodruff was a glorious sign of support to the Brethren gathered in the temple."[60] Similarly, Elder David B. Haight (also of the Twelve) shared his experience: "I was in the temple when President Spencer W. Kimball received the revelation regarding the priesthood. . . . The outpouring of the Spirit [was] . . . so strong that none of us could speak afterwards. We just left quietly to go back to the office. No one could say anything because of the powerful . . . spiritual experience. . . . I was a witness to it."[61]

Elder Bruce R. McConkie described his experience during the revelation in this way: "We all heard the same voice, received the same message, and became personal witnesses that the word received was the mind and will of the Lord."[62] Elder McConkie added:

> When President Kimball finished his prayer, the Lord gave a revelation . . . [to] the First Presidency and the Quorum of the Twelve in a miraculous and marvelous manner, beyond anything that any then present had ever experienced. The revelation came to the President of the Church; it also came to each individual present. . . . President Kimball knew, and each one of us knew, independent of any other person, by direct and personal revelation to us. . . . There was no question whatsoever as to what happened or as to the word and message that came.[63]

President Gordon B. Hinckley also described the experience, saying, "There was a hallowed and sanctified atmosphere in the room. . . . It felt as if a conduit opened between the heavenly throne and the kneeling, pleading prophet of God."[64] Elder L. Tom Perry (of the Quorum of the Twelve Apostles) described what he felt as being "like a wind rushing against [his] face" as he stood in the circle.[65]

Regarding President Lorenzo Snow's efforts to inquire of the Lord (in the Holy of Holies) as to whether he should wait to reconstitute the First Presidency or move forward immediately with the reorganization, he shared the following with his granddaughter, Allie Young Pond:

The Lord Jesus Christ appeared to me at the time of the death of President Woodruff. He instructed me to go right ahead and reorganize the First Presidency of the Church at once and not wait as had been done after the death of the previous presidents, and that I was to succeed President Woodruff. . . . I want you to remember that this is the testimony of your grandfather, that he told you with his own lips that he actually saw the Savior, here in the Temple, and talked with Him face to face.[66]

Like President Snow, when President Russell M. Nelson was seeking to know the Lord's will regarding whom he should choose as his counselors in the First Presidency, he "sequestered" himself "in a *private room* in the temple and sought the Lord's will"—and noted that "the Lord instructed him."[67]

While these are certainly not all the manifestations that have been experienced in the Salt Lake Temple, in its Holy of Holies or in other parts of the temple, they are representative of what has taken place in that sacred building, designed to be a conduit between the heavens and the earth. Each establishes what that holy room is intended to accomplish and what the prophets who enter therein are called to receive on behalf of the world.

Conclusion

The Salt Lake Temple has been called "the most important building of The Church of Jesus Christ of Latter-day Saints"—in part because it represents something more than a traditional temple (in which the Saints seek to redeem their dead).[68] Rather, the Salt Lake Temple stands as a symbol of prophetic authority and the existence of prophets, seers, and revelators who commune with God as in biblical times. Elder B. H. Roberts of the Seventy explained:

> We believe in the revelations of God. One of our articles of faith puts it in this form: "We believe all that God has revealed, all that he does now reveal, and we believe that he will yet reveal many great and important things pertaining to the kingdom of God." We believe that the Church of Christ is within the hearing of God. . . . We feel that this Church of Christ—this Church of ours—is in touch with the Infinite and in tune with the Infinite, that the intelligence and power of God are among its resources; that where

human wisdom comes short, God may be reached.... It is possible for his prophet to ... know the mind and will of God; by going into the *holy of holies*, thus prepared, it is possible, if God will, for him to return with the law of God unto his people, unto his Church, thus making the wisdom and strength of God the wisdom and strength of his Church.[69]

The Holy of Holies of the Salt Lake Temple is a symbol that the heavens are open and that The Church of Jesus Christ of Latter-day Saints is God's Church and kingdom upon the earth today—with living prophets at its head. Indeed, the stained-glass window in the Holy of Holies is a testament to what that room is designed to facilitate. Just as God and Christ appeared to the Prophet of the Restoration, the current prophet has the right and privilege to enter that sacred and set-apart space and seek the mind and will of the Father and Son (see John 14). No doubt, as Joseph's various successors have knelt at the small altar in the center of that room and prayed facing the image of the Father and Son (revealing themselves to the first prophet of this dispensation), each has hoped that a similar theophany might be theirs.

The only currently functioning Holy of Holies in the Church represents the Restoration of the gospel of Jesus Christ in these latter days. It stands as a testament to the existence of prophetic keys. It is a reminder of what President Wilford Woodruff expressed in the dedicatory prayer of the Salt Lake Temple:

> We come before thee with joy and thanksgiving, with spirits jubilant and hearts filled with praise, that thou hast permitted us to see this day for which, during these forty years, we have hoped, and toiled, and prayed, when we can dedicate unto thee this house which we have built unto thy most glorious name ... that thy holy presence may be continually in it; that it may be the abode of thy Well-Beloved Son, our Savior; that the angels who stand before thy face may be the hallowed messengers who shall visit it, bearing to us thy wishes and thy will.[70]

The Salt Lake Temple's Holy of Holies is one of the most important and hallowed spaces on the face of the earth.[71] It is nothing less than a symbol of the fact that the Restoration continues! The heavens are open, and the unchanging God continues to speak. And while none of us are privy to the details of the miraculous visions and revelations received therein, as we watch the workings of God through His living prophets, we can know that the very thing the Holy of Holies represents is true: God speaks to His appointed messengers in these the latter days!

Notes

1. "Wycliffe's 1382 Bible used the phrase 'holi of halowes,' while Milton was first to use the present wording 'holy of holies' in 1641, thirty years after the King James Bible had been published." Richard Cowan, *Temples to Dot the Earth* (Cedar Fort, 1997), 8.
2. "The construction 'Holy of Holies' is a translation of a Hebrew idiom *Qodesh haQodashim*, referring to the inner sanctuary of the Tabernacle or Temple in Jerusalem. In Biblical Hebrew, the Holy of Holies is distinguished from the phrase *most holy* by the definite article; i.e., the room is the *Qodesh haQodashim* or 'Holy of the Holies' and anything else described as most holy is *Qodesh Qodashim*, 'Holy of Holies.'" See "Holy of Holies (LDS Church)," Wikipedia, accessed Jan. 10, 2024, https://en.wikipedia.org/wiki/Holy_of_Holies_(LDS_Church).
3. See Carol Meyers, "Temple, Jerusalem," in *The Anchor Bible Dictionary*, ed. David Noel Freedman, 6 vols. (Doubleday, 1992), 6:358.
4. Bruce R. McConkie, *Mormon Doctrine*, 2nd ed. (Bookcraft, 1979), 547, s.v. "Oracles"; emphasis added. See also James E. Talmage, *Jesus the Christ* (The Church of Jesus Christ of Latter-day Saints, 1981), 76. On a related note, historian John L. Brooke wrote that "temple building, both at Salt Lake and in the outlying centers of St. George, Logan, and Manti" was for the purpose of creating an abode "for the divinity to dwell in." John L. Brooke, *The Refiner's Fire: The Making of Mormon Cosmology, 1644–1844* (Cambridge University Press, 1994), 271–72.
5. See Janne M. Sjodahl, *Temples Ancient and Modern Including an Account of the Laying of the Capstone on the Salt Lake Temple* (Deseret News, n.d.), 3, 4; Boyd K. Packer, *The Holy Temple* (Bookcraft, 1980), 93–94.
6. See Sjodahl, *Temples Ancient and Modern*, 5; Packer, *Holy Temple*, 94.
7. See Sjodahl, *Temples Ancient and Modern*, 13.
8. See Hugh Nibley, *Enoch the Prophet* (Deseret Book and Foundation for Ancient Research and Mormon Studies, 1986), 256–57. "As the house of deity, each Latter-day Saint temple draws from the symbolism of Solomon's Temple and is adorned with the finest materials, standing as a 'physical presence of God's earthly presence.' The temple allows communication with the deity foremost by being set apart as the dwelling of God. For members of the [sic] Church of Jesus Christ of Latter-day Saints, the aspect of communication is a central aspect of their belief." Amanda Buessecker, "Placing the Cardston Temple in Early Mormon Temple Architectural History" (master's thesis, Carleton University, 2020), 33–34.

9. In support of the idea that at least some portion of the Kirtland Temple functioned as a "Holy of Holies," Elder Erastus Snow (of the Quorum of the Twelve Apostles) spoke of seeing "Peter, James and John and Elijah" in "the Holy of Holies" of the Kirtland Temple—which he described as being "in the Arch of the Temple." See Sunday, August 14, 1881, in *Excerpts from the Diary of Charles L. Walker: 1855–1902*, comp. George E. Maycook, (unpublished manuscript, 1969), 39. See also A. Karl Larson and Katharine Miles Larson, eds., *Diary of Charles Lowell Walker*, 2 vols. (Utah State University Press, 1980), 2:563; Joseph Hinerman, *Temple Manifestations* (Mountain Valley, 1974), 37. By "the Arch of the Temple," it is assumed that Elder Snow was referring to the "arched ceiling" of the temple, though he may have meant "the arch framing the west windows" of the temple. See Elwin C. Robison, *The First Mormon Temple* (Brigham Young University Press, 1997), 59, 65, 115, 185, 189–90.
10. Nathan Augustine, "Holy of Holies," Temple Facts, accessed Jan. 10, 2024, https://www.templefacts.org/post/holy-of-holies.
11. Brigham Young, *Manuscript History of Brigham Young 1801–1844*, comp. Elden Jay Watson (n.p., 1968), 158–59, 184, 208, 211, 212, 228, 232, 236–38, 245–46, 255–56, 264, 271; Joseph Hovey, "Autobiography of Joseph Grafton Hovey," typescript, p. 34, L. Tom Perry Special Collections, Harold B. Lee Library, Brigham Young University, Provo, Utah; William Hyde, "Private Journal of William Hyde," p. 16, L. Tom Perry Special Collections.

    Speaking of these very ordinances, and highlighting why this room was different, one source noted, "In the evening I went into the Holy of Holies with Emily my wife where by President Brigham Young we were, according to the holy order of the priesthood, sealed together for time and all eternity, and sealed up into eternal life and against all sin except the sin against the Holy Ghost. May God keep us faithful in his ordinances, Amen." "Norton Jacob, Autobiography: 1804–1847," typescript, January 19, 1846, L. Tom Perry Special Collections. See also Lisle G. Brown, "The Sacred Departments for Temple Work in Nauvoo: The Assembly Room and the Council Chamber," *BYU Studies Quarterly* 19, no. 3 (1979): 373; Devery S. Anderson and Gary James Bergera, eds., *The Nauvoo Endowment Companies, 1845–1846: A Documentary History* (Signature Books, 2005), 377; Lisle G. Brown, "'Temple Pro Tempore': The Salt Lake City Endowment House," *The Journal of Mormon History* 34, no. 4 (Fall 2008): 3.
12. Seventies Record, Book B, cited in Anderson and Bergera, *Nauvoo Endowment Companies*, 377. See also C. Edward Jacob, *The Record of Norton Jacob* (Norton Jacob Family Association, 1949), 15.
13. One source suggested, "Each of these temples [e.g., the St. George Temple, the Logan Temple, the Manti Temple, and the Salt Lake Temple] included a Holy of Holies, which may have also been used for sealing rooms. It was necessary to have such a room set aside for the use of Brigham Young as he traveled from settlement to settlement, and especially because the Salt Lake Temple wasn't completed until long after the other Pioneer Temples were in operation." "Pioneer Temples," MormonWiki, accessed Jan. 10, 2024, https://www.mormonwiki.com/Pioneer_Temples.

14. Ed J. Pinegar (Manti Temple President, 2009–2012), interview by authors, Apr. 23, 2010. See also Augustine, "Holy of Holies"; "Manti Utah Temple," Fandom, accessed Feb. 23, 2004, https://churchofjesuschrist.fandom.com/wiki/Manti_Utah_Temple; "Unique Sealing Rooms," The Trumpet Stone, accessed Feb. 23, 2024, https://thetrumpetstone.blogspot.com/2011/02/unique-sealing-rooms.html; Brian Olson, "Manti Utah Temple Wiki," 3D Latter-day Temples, accessed Jan. 15, 2024, https://photogent.com/manti-utah-temple/wiki/; Scott Vance, "Seer Stones, the Temple and the Urim and Thummim," Mormon Scholar, accessed Jan. 15, 2024, https://mormonscholar.org/early-history/seer-stones-becoming-the-urim-and-thummim/.
15. As of the April 21, 2024, rededication of the Manti Temple (by President Russell M. Nelson), the former Holy of Holies once again became a functioning a sealing room.
16. President Richards was speaking of the ordinance of "Second Anointing."
17. George F. Richards, letter "to the First Presidency and Quorum of the Twelve," August 18, 1949, cited (in its entirety on pp. 281–84) in Devery S. Anderson, *The Development of LDS Temple Worship: 1846–2000* (Signature Books, 2011), 284.
18. See LeGrand Richards, letter, July 5, 1966, cited in Anderson, *LDS Temple Worship*, 359.
19. Tobey R. Orme (Area Temple Facilities Manager), interview by authors, Jan. 24, 2024.
20. See, for example, David S. Andrew and Laurel B. Blank, "The Four Mormon Temples in Utah," *Journal of the Society of Architectural Historians* 30, no. 1 (March 1971): 58, who state, "[There] is in each of the Utah temples a small, elegantly decorated room known as the Holy of Holies, not used in the ordinary temple ritual." See also "Does Each Temple Have a Holy of Holies?," Ask Gramps, accessed Jan. 10, 2024, https://askgramps.org/does-each-temple-have-a-holy-of-holies/; David John Buerger, "'The Fulness of the Priesthood': The Second Anointing in Latter-day Saint Theology and Practice," *Dialogue: A Journal of Mormon Thought* 16, no. 1 (Spring 1983): 43; LeGrand Richards, letter, July 5, 1966, cited in Anderson, *LDS Temple Worship*, 359.
21. Bruce R. McConkie, *Doctrinal New Testament Commentary*, 3 vols. (Bookcraft, 1987–88), 3:588. Elsewhere, Elder McConkie wrote, "'And I saw no temple therein,' John continues, 'for the Lord God Almighty and the Lamb are the temple of it' [Revelation 21:22]. Both God and Christ dwell on the celestial earth and in the Celestial City, and the city and the whole earth (and in the ultimate sense of the word, they are one and the same) are, in fact, a temple. The whole earth in that day will be a Holy of Holies—not a Holy of Holies into which the high priest alone will enter once each year on the day of atonement, there to make atonement for the sins of the people and to pronounce the ineffable name, but a Holy of Holies where all the saints will dwell on all days, and where they, having been redeemed by the blood of the Lamb, will shout praises to God and the Lamb, using all their names, including many we do not even yet know." Bruce R. McConkie, *The Millennial Messiah* (Deseret Book, 1982), 703.

22. Eugene's mother left the Church when he was four years old and reared him as a non–Latter-day Saint. However, because his grandfather was the former President of the Church, and because he had an uncle (Brigham Young Jr.) who was serving in the Quorum of the Twelve at the time of the temple's dedication, President Woodruff granted Eugene a detailed tour the night of April 5, 1893.
23. Talmage wrote the book at the behest of the First Presidency and in response to the fact that the Church was being blackmailed for $100,000 by a person who had broken into the Salt Lake Temple (at night) and taken photos and was threatening to go public with them if the Church didn't meet his demands. Talmage suggested to the Church's First Presidency that they "take the offensive" and publish pictures themselves in a book dedicated to a discussion about what Latter-day Saints do within the walls of their temples. Agreeing with his suggestion, the First Presidency assigned him to write the volume. See David Rolph Seely, "Explaining the Temple to the World: James E. Talmage's Monumental Book, *The House of the Lord*," in *Review of Books on the Book of Mormon* 12, no. 2 (2000): 415–17.
24. See Seely, "Explaining the Temple," 416.
25. Richard O. Cowan, "The Design, Construction, and Role of the Salt Lake Temple," in *Salt Lake City: The Place Which God Prepared*, ed. Scott C. Esplin and Kenneth L. Alford (BYU Religious Studies Center, 2011), 54–55.
26. D. M. McAllister, *A Description of the Great Temple, Salt Lake City, and a Statement Concerning the Purposes for Which It Has Been Built* (Bureau of Information, 1904), 11. Duncan McAllister was the temple recorder for the Salt Lake Temple from 1893 until 1916 and the recorder for the St. George Temple from 1916 until 1918.
27. See Salt Lake Temple Architectural Blueprint Holy of Holies Floorplan, December 6, 1972. See also "Salt Lake Temple Symbolic Progression," The Trumpet Stone, accessed Feb. 23, 2024, https://thetrumpetstone.blogspot.com/2011/02/salt-lake-temple-symbolic-progression.html; C. Mark Hamilton, *The Salt Lake Temple: A Monument to a People*, 5th ed. (University Services, 1983), 102.
28. James E. Talmage, *The House of the Lord: A Study of Holy Sanctuaries, Ancient and Modern* (Bookcraft, 1962), 193. See also Hamilton, *Salt Lake Temple*, 122; Eugene Young, "Inside the New Mormon Temple," *Harper's Weekly*, May 27, 1893, 510.
29. See McAllister, *Great Temple*, 11.
30. See Talmage, *House of the Lord*, 192–93.
31. Talmage, *House of the Lord*, 193. See also Young, "New Mormon Temple," 510.
32. Talmage, *House of the Lord*, 193. See also McAllister, *Great Temple*, 11.
33. See Talmage, *House of the Lord*, 193; Lysle R. Cahoon, "Holy of Holies," *Encyclopedia of Mormonism*, ed. Daniel H. Ludlow, 4 vols. (Macmillan, 1992), 2:651; McAllister, *Great Temple*, 11.
34. See 1893 blueprint drawing by Joseph Don Carlos Young. See also Hamilton, *Salt Lake Temple*, 78.

35. Dr. Joseph Carbone, interview by authors, Feb. 29, 2024.
36. See Talmage, *House of the Lord*, 193; Young, "New Mormon Temple," 510; Cahoon, "Holy of Holies," 2:651; McAllister, *Great Temple*, 11.
37. See Cahoon, "Holy of Holies," 2:651.
38. Young, "New Mormon Temple," 510.
39. Talmage, *House of the Lord*, 193. See also McAllister, *Great Temple*, 11; Young, "New Mormon Temple," 510.
40. McAllister, *Great Temple*, 11–12. See also Young, "New Mormon Temple," 510; Talmage, *House of the Lord*, 193.
41. Dr. Joseph Carbone, interview by authors, Feb. 29, 2024. In the opinion of the authors of this paper, the original floor had an almost three-dimensional feel, arranged in such a way that it visually appeared as though the floor was emerging upward, suggesting the idea of ascension into God's presence.
42. Dr. Joseph Carbone, interview by authors, Feb. 29, 2024.
43. See Talmage, *House of the Lord*, 193; Young, "New Mormon Temple," 511.
44. See Talmage, *House of the Lord*, 193.
45. See McAllister, *Great Temple*, 12. See also Talmage, *House of the Lord*, 193. The back side of the stained-glass window can actually be viewed from an "anteroom" built on the back side of the Holy of Holies. See the 1893 blueprint drawing by Joseph Don Carlos Young, in Hamilton, *Salt Lake Temple*, 78.
46. See McAllister, *Great Temple*, 12; Joyce Athay Janetski, "Stained Glass Windows: A Latter-day Saint Legacy," *Ensign*, Jan. 1981, 34–41; Joyce Athay Janetski, "Louis Comfort Tiffany: Stained Glass in Utah," *Utah Preservation/Restoration: A Publication for the Preservationist* 3 (1981): 20–21. On September 20, 1892, Brigham Young's son (Joseph Don Carlos Young, who served as Church architect from 1887 to 1893) sent a letter to Tiffany and Co. describing what the stained-glass window should look like. In many ways, Young's letter reads like an early missionary tract, telling the story of the First Vision and describing the spiritual impact the window should have on those who would view it—even though the number of viewers (in this era of limited photography) would have been expected to be quite low. See Richard G. Oman, "'Ye Shall See the Heavens Open': Portrayal of the Divine and the Angelic in Latter-day Saint Art," *BYU Studies Quarterly* 35, no. 4 (1995–1996): 116–18.
47. See Talmage, *House of the Lord*, 194; Cahoon, "Holy of Holies," 2:651.
48. See Young, "New Mormon Temple," 511; John P. Hatch, "From Prayer to Visitation: Reexamining Lorenzo Snow's Vision of Jesus Christ in the Salt Lake Temple," *Journal of Mormon History* 42, no. 3 (July 2016): 155, 157, see also 138; Francis M. Gibbons, *Spencer W. Kimball: Resolute Disciple, Prophet of God* (Deseret Book, 2009), 293–94; Gordon B. Hinckley, "Priesthood Restoration," *Ensign*, Oct. 1988, 70; F. Burton Howard, *Marion G. Romney: His Life and Faith* (Bookcraft, 1988), 239.

Significantly, Solomon's temple had at the center of its Holy of Holies the ark of the covenant, and the Salt Lake Temple has at the center of its Holy of Holies an altar, both of which are symbols of God, Christ, and sacrifice. One source has claimed that the current altar in the Salt Lake Temple's Holy of

Holies has "wheels" and is sometimes "stored" in an adjoining "accouchement room" when space is needed for "other activities" carried out in the Holy of Holies. Dr. Joseph Carbone, interview by authors, Feb. 29, 2024. The photo of the Holy of Holies (in Talmage's 1912 *The House of the Lord*) has no altar at the center of the room but a small table instead. This *may* confirm the aforementioned claim about a "removable" altar on "wheels."

49. Prior to their arrival in the Utah Territory, Church leaders had dedicated a lot in Independence, Missouri, for a temple complex (consisting of twenty-four buildings), but those were never built. The Saints had also built and dedicated (on March 27, 1836) the Kirtland Ohio Temple. In Far West, Missouri, and Adam-ondi-Ahman, Missouri, the Church had dedicated temple lots, but those temples were never built. In Nauvoo, Illinois, the Church constructed and then dedicated a temple (on May 1–3, 1846), which they ultimately had to abandon as they migrated west.

50. The Salt Lake Endowment House was dedicated on May 5, 1855; the St. George temple on April 6–8, 1877; the Logan Temple on May 17–19, 1884; the Manti Temple on May 17, 1888; and the Salt Lake Temple on April 6–24, 1893. While the Endowment House was dedicated and set apart for temple ordinances, it was not "officially" one of the temples of the Church but served as a temporary structure to be used until actual temples could be constructed.

51. Hamilton, *Salt Lake Temple*, 141.

52. Hamilton, *Salt Lake Temple*, 141. While Hamilton is correct about the iconic nature of this temple, he also suggested the following: "It is significant that the Salt Lake Temple was designed from the outset *to function solely in the capacity of sacred space*; because it is here where God could dwell within walls dedicated for that purpose." Ibid. While on its face, the Salt Lake Temple may *look* like the first temple to *not* be a multipurpose temple (akin to Kirtland), the first to "function solely in the capacity of sacred space," the fact of the matter is that because it has counsel rooms for the First Presidency, the Twelve, and the Presidency of the Seventy (in addition to an Assembly Hall), in many ways, the Salt Lake Temple *does* function like the old Kirtland Temple, as it is both administrative and "sacred space" combined. Yes, there are limitations as to who can enter the Salt Lake Temple. Nonetheless, its administrative function is *undeniably* part of its purpose in the Church today.

53. Hamilton, *Salt Lake Temple*, 104.

54. Hamilton, *Salt Lake Temple*, 104, 108.

55. Talmage, *House of the Lord*, 194; see also 274–76.

56. Packer, *Holy Temple*, 4.

57. Cahoon, "Holy of Holies," 2:651.

58. In relation to the Salt Lake Temple being the "most holy space upon the face of the earth," when renovations were performed on the temple (in the early 1960s), the blueprints associated with that renovation referred to the Holy of Holies as the temple's "special room." Dr. Joseph Carbone, interview with authors, Feb. 29, 2024.

59. Though President Kimball spent many hours in the Holy of Holies praying about this matter, when the First Presidency and Quorum of the Twelve

assembled (on Thursday, June 1, 1978) to unitedly pray about the matter, those present when the revelation on priesthood was received were assembled in the "Council Room of the First Presidency and the Twelve Apostles"—not in the Holy of Holies. See Hamilton, *Salt Lake Temple*, 79, 105, 130.

60. See "Elder Richards, Missionary, Goes to his Rest," *Deseret News*, Jan. 15, 1983, B2. This event was confirmed both by members of Elder LeGrand Richards's family and by Elder Boyd K. Packer in his remarks at Elder Richards's funeral. See Elaine Cannon, *The Truth about Angels* (Bookcraft, 1996), 32, 39.
61. David B. Haight, "This Work Is True," *Ensign*, May 1996, 23.
62. Bruce R. McConkie, "The New Revelation," in *Priesthood* (Deseret Book, 1981), 128.
63. Bruce R. McConkie, "All Are Alike Unto God," in *The 1978 C.E.S. Symposium on the Book of Mormon* (The Church of Jesus Christ of Latter-day Saints, 1979), 4.
64. Gordon B. Hinckley, "Priesthood Restoration," *Ensign*, Oct. 1988, 70; see also Stephen E. Robinson and H. Dean Garrett, *A Commentary on the Doctrine and Covenants*, 4 vols. (Deseret Book, 2000–2005), 4:324.
65. L. Tom Perry, conversation with faculty at the Institute of Religion adjacent to Utah Valley University, Jan. 15, 2010.
66. Cowan, *Temples to Dot the Earth*, 117–18. See LeRoi C. Snow, "An Experience of My Father's," *Improvement Era*, Sept. 1933, 677, 679. While President Snow's son, LeRoi, wrote the account quoted herein, he indicated that he received it from his niece, Allie Young Pond; if she wrote down the story herself, her version of it has not survived.
67. Russell M. Nelson, "Revelation for the Church, Revelation for Our Lives," *Ensign*, May 2018, 94–95; emphasis added. The term "private room" almost certainly refers to the Holy of Holies.
68. Hamilton, *Salt Lake Temple*, 204. "Brigham Young . . . saw the entire city [of Salt Lake] as the theocratic center of the Church with the Temple as its spiritual center. Historic events prevented it from becoming a theocratically governed city. The Temple, however, does remain the spiritual center of The Church of Jesus Christ of Latter-day Saints as the envisioned 'ensign to the nations from afar.'" Hamilton, *Salt Lake Temple*, 182.
69. B. H. Roberts, *Defense of the Faith and the Saints*, 2 vols. (Deseret News Press, 1912), 2:456; emphasis added.
70. Hamilton, *Salt Lake Temple*, 210.
71. While certain sacred spaces associated with the revelations of the Prophet Joseph Smith are reverenced as holy by members of the Church, when one considers the fact that *every one* of Joseph's successors (other than Brigham Young) has knelt at the altar in the Holy of Holies of the Salt Lake Temple and sought the will of the Lord, there are ways in which the flagship temple's Holy of Holies surpasses even the Sacred Grove because of the sheer number of revelations given therein as part of the ongoing Restoration of the gospel of Jesus Christ. We cannot emphasize enough how important this set-apart room has been in moving forward the work of God.

The Revelation on the Priesthood Received in the Temple

Mary Jane Woodger & Emily Lambert

OVER ITS DECADES OF OPERATION, THE SALT LAKE TEMPLE HAS served as a sacred space where patrons have received personal revelation and direction. Perhaps the widest-reaching revelation ever received took place on June 1, 1978, resulting in Official Declaration 2. The declaration, and the revelation that prompted it, "extend[ed] to every worthy member of the Church all the privileges and blessings which the gospel affords" (Official Declaration 2). Despite the current reality of an integrated Church, "for much of its history—from the mid-1800s until 1978—the Church did not ordain men of Black African descent to its priesthood or allow Black men or women to participate in temple endowment or sealing ordinances. The Church was established in 1830, during an era of great racial division in the United States. At the time, many people of African descent lived in slavery, and racial distinctions and prejudice were not just common but customary among white Americans. Those realities, though unfamiliar and disturbing today, influenced all aspects of people's lives, including their religion."[1]

During the time of the restriction, "'promises [were] made by the prophets and presidents of the Church . . . that at some time, in God's eternal plan, all of our brethren who are worthy [could] receive the priesthood.' . . . Although these prophets yearned for the day the Lord would extend the priesthood to all worthy males, it was through President Spencer W. Kimball that the Lord brought that desire to fruition."[2]

Precursor to the Revelation

In the years leading up to the revelation on the priesthood, the matter of extending the priesthood to all worthy males was constantly on President Kimball's mind. Family and friends remember his tireless efforts as he prayerfully asked for guidance. President Kimball himself shared how he sought revelation in the Salt Lake Temple:

> Day after day, and especially on Saturdays and Sundays when there were no organizations [sessions] in the temple, I went there when I could be alone. I was very humble. . . . I was searching for this. . . . I wanted to be sure. . . . I had a great deal to fight . . . myself, largely, because I had grown up with this thought that Negroes should not have the priesthood and I was prepared to go all the rest of my life until my death and fight for it and defend it as it was.[3]

President Kimball had not suddenly gained an interest in the priesthood restriction in 1978; rather, it had been a consistent focus of his long life before he received the revelation:

> He was being prepared, along with Church members of African descent and others, for the revelation in 1978. . . . During President Kimball's apostolic ministry, "his heart had gone out to faithful priesthood–denied people wherever they resided in the world." He was well known among the Genesis Group—a group of black members of the Church in the Salt Lake Valley. After attending the Genesis Christmas social in the 1970s, acting President Boyd K. Packer of the Quorum of the Twelve remembers President Kimball's words, "They need our help, they need our prayers and our blessings, and they need our attention. They really need our attention."

Taking his own advice, President Kimball began to earnestly give members of the Genesis Group and black Latter-day Saints across the world his attention. The Holy Ghost motivated him to seek revelation on this matter. He prepared himself in the same way all who seek revelation and blessings should prepare. He began an exhaustive personal study of the scriptures as well as statements of Church leaders since Joseph Smith, and he asked other General Authorities to share their personal feelings relative to the long-standing Church policy. Church leaders [had] discussed the subject "at length on numerous occasions in the preceding weeks and months."[4]

President Kimball constantly desired to be in the Salt Lake Temple when seeking revelation. For instance, his son Edward L. Kimball tells us, "On returning from the airport in February 1978 after one of his trips, Spencer asked the driver to let him off at the temple and sent Camilla home alone. 'I want to go to the temple for a while,' he said. 'I'll get a way home.' Some days he went more than once [to the Salt Lake Temple], often alone. Sometimes he changed into temple clothing; he always took off his shoes. He obtained a key that gave him access to the temple night or day without having to involve anyone else."[5]

As he sought revelation, he also studied the issue, requesting reports, opinions, accounts, and information from other General Authorities, scholars, and Latter-day Saints personally affected. He also assembled a notebook with article clippings and information on the subject.

His own personal witness came gradually—and with great effort on his part—before the revelation was given to the rest of the Apostles. His actions set a pattern and example of how to receive revelation:

> Over time, through the many days in the temple and through the sleepless hours of the night, praying and turning over in his mind all the consequences, perplexities, and criticisms that a decision to extend priesthood would involve, Spencer gradually found "all those complications and concerns dwindling in significance." They did not disappear but seemed to decline in importance. Despite his preconceptions and his allegiance to the past, a swelling certainty grew that a change in policy was what the Lord wanted.

"There grew slowly a deep, abiding impression to go forward with the change."⁶

We Were Not Alone

On May 5, 1978, amid President Kimball's inquiries, the General Authorities' weekly meeting in the Salt Lake Temple included a discussion about the priesthood restriction. After the meeting, Elder LeGrand Richards asked to say a few words:

> Brethren, I have something to tell you. A little while ago, I saw a man seated above the organ there and he looked just like that. (He gestured toward President Wilford Woodruff's portrait which hangs in the room.) . . . I saw him just as clearly as I see any of you brethren. . . . He was dressed in a white suit and was seated in an armchair. I thought at the time that the only reason I was privileged to see him was probably that I was the only one there who had ever seen President Woodruff while he was upon the Earth. I had heard him dedicate the Salt Lake Temple and I had heard him give his last sermon in the Salt Lake Tabernacle before he died. I thought it wonderful that the Lord could project, without any mechanical means, the likeness of a man long since dead.⁷

One must wonder why the Lord would have President Wilford Woodruff appear to Elder LeGrand Richards at this specific time. The connection may be that President Woodruff also dealt with an issue in which revelation was needed that would greatly affect members of the Church. He was the prophet who announced the first Official Declaration, ending polygamy, and the one who dedicated the Salt Lake Temple. His visit, it would seem, was divinely providential.

A Good, Warm Feeling

In the days leading up to the revelation, it became increasingly clear that a change was on its way. First Presidency secretary Francis M. Gibbons recorded:

> On Tuesday, May 30, 1978, President Kimball read to his counselors a tentative statement he had written in longhand removing all priesthood restrictions from Blacks except those restrictions as to worthiness that rest upon all alike. He said that he had "a good,

warm feeling" about it. There was a lengthy review of the statements of past leaders about the restrictions on Blacks. It was decided that this aspect of the matter should be researched in detail. Elder G. Homer Durham, who was serving as the Church historian, was asked to do this.[8]

President Kimball was doing everything in his power to prepare to receive and give further revelation, and his efforts would soon be rewarded.

In the Upper Rooms of the Salt Lake Temple

Weekly meetings of the general Church leaders in the upper room of the Salt Lake Temple are certainly filled with the Spirit. The first Thursday of each month has been designated as a time when members of the Quorum of the Twelve meet together in a spirit of prayer and fasting. In a 1979 address, Elder N. Eldon Tanner described the room as a place where "one experiences a special spiritual feeling, and at times senses the presence of some of these great leaders who have gone on before. Portraits of the twelve Presidents of the Church, and of Hyrum [Smith], the Patriarch, hang on the walls. There are also paintings of the Savior at the Sea of Galilee where he called some of his apostles, and others portraying his crucifixion and his ascension. Here we are reminded of the many great leaders who have sat in this council room, and under the direction of the Lord great decisions were made." In the same talk, Elder Tanner also described the procedure of their meetings, saying, "As the First Presidency enters this room . . . on Thursday mornings, we shake hands with all members of the Twelve, then change to our temple robes. We sing, kneel in prayer, and then join in a prayer circle at the altar, after which we change to our street clothes."[9] It was in one of these meetings on June 1, 1978, that a marvelous revelation was received.

President Kimball Prayed Fervently

Elder David B. Haight recalled of that June 1, 1978, meeting:

President Kimball . . . suggested that we have our prayer at the altar. Usually, he asked one of us to lead in prayer; however, on this day he asked, "Would you mind if I be voice at the altar today?" . . .

The prophet of God pour[ed] out his heart, pleading eloquently for the Lord to make his mind and will known to his servant, Spencer W. Kimball. The prophet pleaded that he would be given the necessary direction which could expand the Church throughout the world by offering the fullness of the everlasting gospel to all men, based solely upon their personal worthiness without reference to race or color.[10]

His heartfelt prayer, and the revelation that followed, left a deep impression on all those in attendance.

President Thomas S. Monson remembered that "[President Kimball] implored the Lord for light and knowledge on this issue which has such far-reaching consequences. It was a source of great comfort to the Brethren to hear his humble pleadings as he sought guidance in his lofty calling."[11] His prayer echoed within the walls of the Salt Lake Temple, where so many before and after him would also plead with the Lord for guidance and revelation.

All Present Had the Same Experience

What happened next was described by some present as a Pentecostal outpouring and was experienced by all thirteen men at the meeting that day. In attendance were Spencer W. Kimball, N. Eldon Tanner, Marion G. Romney, Ezra Taft Benson, LeGrand Richards, Howard W. Hunter, Gordon B. Hinckley, Thomas S. Monson, Boyd K. Packer, Marvin J. Ashton, Bruce R. McConkie, L. Tom Perry, and David B. Haight. Only two members of the Quorum of the Twelve were missing: Elder Mark E. Peterson, who was on assignment at the time in South America, and Elder Delbert L. Stapley, who was in the hospital.[12] The thirteen present experienced the same thing at the same exact time.

Though it is difficult to describe such a spiritual revelation with mortal words, some of the members of the Twelve have attempted to describe what took place in the sacred edifice that day. President Ezra Taft Benson explained, "Following the prayer, we experienced the sweetest spirit of unity and conviction that I have ever experienced. . . . We took each other in our arms, we were so impressed with the sweet spirit that was in evidence. Our bosoms burned with the righteousness of the decision we had made. Thank God for the inspired leadership and the great and enduring principle of revelation. What a blessing it is to be associated with this, the greatest work in all the world."[13]

Elder Bruce R. McConkie observed, "The Spirit of the Lord rested mightily upon us all; we felt something akin to what happened on the day of Pentecost and at the dedication of the Kirtland Temple. From the midst of eternity, the voice of God, conveyed by the power of the Spirit, spoke to His prophet. . . . And we all heard the same voice, received the same message, and became personal witnesses that the word received was the mind and will and voice of the Lord."[14]

President Gordon B. Hinckley also gave an account and described the feelings he experienced that day:

> There was a hallowed and sanctified atmosphere in the room. For me, it felt as if a conduit opened between the heavenly throne and the kneeling, pleading prophet of God who was joined by his brethren. The Spirit of God was there. And by the power of the Holy Ghost there came to that prophet an assurance that the thing for which he prayed was right, that the time had come, and that now the wondrous blessings of the priesthood should be extended to worthy men everywhere regardless of lineage.
>
> Every man in that circle, by the power of the Holy Ghost, knew the same thing. It was a quiet and sublime occasion. There was not the sound "as of a rushing mighty wind" [;] there were not "cloven tongues like as of fire" (Acts 2:2–3) as there had been on the Day of Pentecost. But there was a Pentecostal spirit, for the Holy Ghost was there. No voice audible to our physical ears was heard. But the voice of the Spirit whispered with certainty into our minds and our very souls. It was for us, at least for me personally, as I imagine it was with Enos, who said concerning his remarkable experience, "And while I was thus struggling in the spirit, behold, the voice of the Lord came into my mind" (Enos 1:10).[15]

In President Hinckley's description, we can see wording that might also describe the countless revelations that Latter-day Saints have received in the Salt Lake Temple after they too have struggled to know the will of the Lord. Bringing forth this revelation was a struggle. The revelation that blessed Latter-day Saints for generations to come was not a sudden burst of unexpected insight but something prayed for and wrestled with for years, both by the General Authorities and by rank-and-file members. Other General Authorities present in the upper room of the Salt Lake Temple echoed the experience.

Elder L. Tom Perry described the revelation as "the most spiritual and significant experience in the Brethren's Thursday Temple meetings in his thirty-eight years of attending them" and declared, "We were not alone."[16] Elder Marvin J. Ashton concurred and emphasized the importance of earnestly seeking revelation and direction, saying, "The 1978 revelation on priesthood involved the most intense spiritual impression I've ever felt, but that also came only after weeks, months, even years of prayer and searching on the part of the First Presidency and the Twelve."[17] What a powerful representation this is of the countless Latter-day Saints who also seek revelation of their own in the Salt Lake Temple.

Elder David B. Haight, then the most junior of the Apostles, offered additional insight: "In that room within the Lord's holy house, we were witnesses that the answer came to the Lord's prophet. The spirit touched each of our hearts with the same message in the same way. Each was witness to a transcendent heavenly event."[18] In another account, Elder Haight described, "I was in the room . . . and was a witness to an outpouring of the Spirit. It was so powerful that none of us could speak. We felt a presence in the room. We didn't hear a voice; we only felt the Spirit. . . . The Spirit was so powerful after President Kimball's prayer that we went quietly to our dressing rooms, and no one said a word. We went back to our offices, and no one spoke."[19]

To All the World

Official press releases were sent out the next week, and from within the Church, the response was "overwhelmingly positive." Carol Lawrence-Costley, a Black member who had joined the Church prior to the 1978 revelation and who recently served on the Young Women General Advisory Council, recalled her experience learning of the revelation. She described her "screams of joy" and remarked that the announcement "was almost unbelievable." She went on to say, "A deep sense of gratitude came over me for the efforts of President Kimball, who took the time to wrestle with the matter of the priesthood and bring it forth to the rest of the brethren."[20]

Shortly after the announcement, wards began to set apart Black Latter-day Saints as elders. When it came to President Kimball's attention that Ruffin Bridgeford, president of the Genesis Group, had not yet been set apart a week after the announcement, the following occurred:

> Elder Packer, discussing the situation with President Kimball, asked whether Brother Bridgeforth might properly be ordained a high priest rather than an elder in light of his long and faithful service. After pondering the question, President Kimball said, "Yes, that's right. You do that." After Brother Bridgeforth was ordained, he asked Elder Packer to give his wheelchair-bound wife, Helena, a priesthood blessing. Elder Packer later recalled, "I laid my hands on her head and just as I was to speak, I thought, 'Ruffin, you can now give this blessing.' And when he began that blessing—and he needed no coaching—by the authority of the Melchizedek Priesthood, that . . . was a moment in Church history."[21]

OFFICIAL DECLARATION 2

On September 30, 1978, N. Eldon Tanner read the formal announcement in general conference:

> In early June of this year, the First Presidency announced that a revelation had been received by President Spencer W. Kimball extending priesthood and temple blessings to all worthy male members of the Church. President Kimball has asked that I advise the conference that after he had received this revelation, which came to him after extended meditation and prayer in the sacred rooms of the holy temple, he presented it to his counselors, who accepted it and approved it. It was then presented to the Quorum of the Twelve Apostles, who unanimously approved it, and was subsequently presented to all other General Authorities, who likewise approved it unanimously. (Official Declaration 2)

THE BLESSINGS OF THE REVELATION

Shortly after the announcement of Official Declaration 2 giving all worthy members temple blessings, the São Paulo Brazil Temple was dedicated. As a result of this revelation, many who would have otherwise not had access to this temple received their temple blessings. As the incubator for the revelation on the priesthood, the Salt Lake Temple was at the heart of a change that has blessed the lives of countless people through missionary work undertaken, temple ordinances received, blessings given, and covenants made.

Notes

1. Gospel Topics Essays, "Race and the Priesthood," Gospel Library.
2. Mary Jane Woodger, "Revelation Attitudes: The Coming Forth of Official Declaration 2," *Religious Educator* 3, no. 2 (2002): 186.
3. Edward L. Kimball, "Spencer W. Kimball and the Revelation on Priesthood," *BYU Studies Quarterly* 47, no. 2 (2008).
4. Woodger, "Revelation Attitudes," 187–88.
5. Spencer W. Kimball, "Revelation on Priesthood."
6. Spencer W. Kimball, "Revelation on Priesthood."
7. Lucille Tate, *LeGrand Richards: Beloved Apostle* (Bookcraft, 1982), 291–92.
8. Woodger, "Revelation Attitudes," 196–97.
9. N. Eldon Tanner, "The Administration of the Church," *Ensign*, Nov. 1979, 42–48.
10. E. Dale LeBaron, "Revelation on the Priesthood, Thirty-Five Years Later," *Religious Educator* 14, no. 3 (2013): 121–35.
11. Carol Lawrence-Costley, Ahmad S. Corbitt, Edward Dube, and Tracy Y. Browning, *Stay Thou Nearby: Reflections on the 1978 Revelation on the Priesthood* (Deseret Book, 2023).
12. John L. Hart, "Make Giants Out of All Missionaries," *Church News*, Jan. 24, 1998.
13. Sheri Dew, *Ezra Taft Benson: A Biography* (Deseret Book, 1997), 457.
14. R. Scott Lloyd, "Revelation Rewarded Those Who Waited," *Church News*, Dec. 18, 1999.
15. Gordon B. Hinckley, "Priesthood Restoration," *Ensign*, Oct. 1988, 70.
16. Lawrence-Costley et al., *Stay Thou Nearby*, 47.
17. Breck England, "Elder Marvin J. Ashton: Friend to Prisoners and Prophets," *Ensign*, July 1978.
18. Lucille Tate, *The Life Story of an Apostle* (Deseret Book, 1987), 278.
19. John L. Hart, "Make Giants out of All Missionaries," *Church News*, Jan. 24, 1998.
20. Lawrence-Costley et al., *Stay Thou Nearby*, 16–17.
21. Kimball, "Revelation on Priesthood."

Writing *Jesus the Christ* in the Salt Lake Temple

Leah Darby

BETWEEN 1904 AND 1906, JAMES E. TALMAGE DELIVERED A SERIES OF university Sunday School addresses at Brigham Young Academy titled "Jesus the Christ." In 1905 Talmage received a formal request from the First Presidency of the Church to compile his lectures into a book.[1] Talmage wrote in his journal that "compliance of the request [would] require much time as not half the lectures have been delivered and not a line of one of them written, except as class notes."[2] It was not until 1914, however, that Talmage began his work on the manuscript. On September 14, 1914, Talmage wrote that while his work on the book had been delayed, he had recently been asked "to prepare the matter for the book with as little delay as possible."[3]

Many believe that *Jesus the Christ* was written under direct revelation from God, but this is a result of misunderstanding why Talmage wrote this book in the Salt Lake Temple. After being urged by the First Presidency to devote his time to completing the manuscript as quickly as possible, Talmage was unable to write "neither in [his] comfortable office nor in the convenient study room at home" due to outside distractions and disruptions.[4] Because of the importance of this book, the Church provided Talmage with a room in the Salt Lake Temple where he could write free of interruption. The room was assigned to Talmage for all writing on Church matters that he did throughout the rest of his life. Talmage wrote of the Spirit he felt in the temple while working on the manuscript, but he did not write under direct revelation. The Spirit of the temple, however, was one of the most important factors in the writing of this inspired volume.

After beginning his work on the manuscript on September 14, 1914, Talmage dedicated almost every waking minute to writing. When he was not performing Church duties, Talmage was writing. On November 9, just under two months after beginning his work, he wrote in his journal that he had "devoted every spare hour to that labor and have at present in written form though not all in revised condition twenty chapters."[5] Talmage's wife, Maia, and his children felt, in a way, that they had lost their husband and father as he devoted all his time and energy to the writing of this book.[6] Despite his commitment to the swift completion of *Jesus the Christ*, Talmage never wrote on Sundays. On February 28, 1915, he wrote in his journal, "[I] spent the greater part of the day in the Temple, as I have spent every day on which I have been free from appointments for months past."[7]

Another popular myth regarding Talmage's work is that he lived in the temple while writing *Jesus the Christ*. While he spent the majority of his time there, he never slept at the temple. Each morning, Talmage left home early carrying a satchel, similar to the black bags used by doctors, filled with "several slices of homemade bread, buttered; two hard-cooked eggs; celery and fresh fruits in season; and a wedge of 'sharp' cheddar cheese."[8] He would get home around midnight to eat dinner and get a few hours of rest. Talmage worked on the manuscript every waking minute that he could. His notes in his journal indicate that even on holidays he would sneak away after the festivities to write.

Throughout his book-writing process, Talmage met regularly with the First Presidency. He would read completed chapters of the book to them as well as discuss other matters related to the book. Although the First Presidency was anxious for *Jesus the Christ* to be written, they were unsure of the book's exact audience. On November 19, 1914, Talmage wrote that he read aloud several chapters of the book to help the First Presidency determine "whether the book would be properly suited for the lower or higher grades in the theological department."⁹ It was decided that the book would be targeted to the general public—it would not be adapted into a textbook for students. Talmage met with the First Presidency a total of eighteen times to read sections of the manuscript. His last meeting took place on June 24, 1915, and the book went to press immediately after. By August 7, the printing was "well advanced."[10]

Upon completing the writing for *Jesus the Christ*, the first thing he told his wife, Maia, was that "it was the outstanding book of all he had written, or would ever write."[11] Maia and his two youngest children shared that they sensed a deep joy and satisfaction surrounding James when he first returned home after finishing the manuscript.[12]

On August 14, 1915, the Church released a statement in the *Deseret Evening News* concerning the release of the book. A description of the work was provided along with the request that it be "read and studied by the Latter-day Saints . . . especially for use in our Church schools, as also for the advanced theological classes in Sunday schools and priesthood quorums, for the instruction of our missionaries, and for general reading."[13] The Church published this message in hopes of encouraging Church scholars, organizations, and teachers to include the material from this book in their lessons. The first copies of *Jesus the Christ* were released on September 9, 1915, less than a year after Talmage began writing in the Salt Lake Temple.

Just one month after the initial release of *Jesus the Christ*, a second edition of the book was commissioned. More than half the first edition had been sold, and with material from the book being implemented into religious classes, there was a great need for a second printing. The *Deseret News* reported that demand for the book came from all parts of the West.[14] On December 10, 1915, the *Deseret Evening News* reported that due to the great success of the first edition, limited editions of *Jesus the Christ* were to be printed "on India paper and bound in three styles, Morocco, divinity circled gold edges, flexible binding."[15] These special editions of the book were intended specifically for the holiday season.

Talmage attributed both the timely completion of the manuscript as well as inspiration for the subject matter to his writing it in the Salt Lake Temple. On the day he finished writing *Jesus the Christ*, Talmage wrote in his journal that "had it not been that I was privileged to do this work in the Temple it would be at present far from completion. I have felt the inspiration of the place."[16] All the writing done for the book took place in the Salt Lake Temple. Not only did the temple provide the quiet, distraction-free environment Talmage needed in order to write the manuscript without delay, but it also allowed him to be more in touch with the Spirit as he wrote.

NOTES

1. James E. Talmage, *The Essential James E. Talmage* (Signature Books, 1997), 163.
2. *James E. Talmage*, 163.
3. James E. Talmage journal, 1914, MSS 229, series 1, box 5, folder 1, L. Tom Perry Special Collections, Harold B. Lee Library, Brigham Young University, Provo, Utah.
4. James E. Talmage journal, 1914, folder 1, L. Tom Perry Special Collections.
5. James E. Talmage journal, 1914, folder 1, L. Tom Perry Special Collections.
6. John R. Talmage, *The Talmage Story* (Bookcraft, 1972), 185.
7. James E. Talmage journal, 1915, MSS 229, series 1, box 5, folder 2, L. Tom Perry Special Collections.
8. Talmage, *Talmage Story*, 182.
9. James E. Talmage journal, 1914, folder 1, L. Tom Perry Special Collections.
10. James E. Talmage journal, 1915, folder 1, L. Tom Perry Special Collections.
11. Talmage, *Talmage Story*, 185.
12. Talmage, *Talmage Story*, 185.
13. James E. Talmage journal, 1915, folder 2, L. Tom Perry Special Collections.
14. James E. Talmage journal, 1915, folder 3, MSS 229, series 1, box 5, folder 3, L. Tom Perry Special Collections.
15. James E. Talmage journal, 1915, folder 3, L. Tom Perry Special Collections.
16. James E. Talmage journal, 1915, folder 2, L. Tom Perry Special Collections.

The Security of the Sealing Power of the Priesthood

Andrew C. Skinner

My attention has long been riveted on the sealing power of the holy priesthood. It first developed because of my experience in the Salt Lake Temple in 1961. In June of that year, my family and I were sealed together for eternity. We traveled from our home in Colorado to Salt Lake City to enter what I could feel was a special place, even at age ten. I remember the day as one of exceptional happiness. A feeling of tremendous security washed over me as my father, mother, sister, and I knelt around a temple altar, along with an older woman, who I had never seen before, acting as proxy for an infant sister of mine who had died three days after her birth. *Happy, secure, safe,* and *stable* are words I use now to describe what I felt then. Ironically, it was the first time I remember seeing my mother and father weeping openly, which was disconcerting to me at the time. I have since learned that my parents' deep feelings stemmed from the same source—joy over becoming a family forever, including a sister I had never known and who my mother had held in her arms only a few times.

That was my first experience in any temple. I remember much of it vividly. For this reason, I suppose, the Salt Lake Temple has always been "my" temple, so to speak. I now know that the promises contained in the sealing ceremony are conditional upon worthiness. But that understanding was not part of my consciousness as a ten-year-old boy; I simply felt secure that day that I would never be without a family. Nor did I have any inkling of events that would overwhelm us four years later when my father passed away unexpectedly and my trust in, and reliance on, the memory of our temple experience would help me get through some dark days.

Fulness of the Priesthood

The sealing power that was put into effect in the Salt Lake Temple on behalf of my family that June day in 1961 is a very real power, just like forces of matter and energy that operate in the universe but are invisible to the naked eye. It is the power to bind or weld individual families together for eternity so that no other power or force can separate members of those families from each other if they remain faithful to the covenants associated with the sealing ordinances. In addition, the sealing ordinances also bind each of us to the larger family of our heavenly parents. President Joseph Fielding Smith stated that "sealings [are] essential to membership in God's family. . . . Why do we go into temples to be sealed, husbands and wives, and children to parents, and why are we commanded to have this work done, not only for ourselves, but also to be sealed to our fathers and mothers, and their fathers and mothers before them, back as far as we can go? Because we want to belong to that great family of God which is in heaven."[1]

The sealing power is a function of the fulness of the Melchizedek Priesthood, the highest authority given to humankind on earth by God. The sealing power or fulness of the priesthood is guarded by God very carefully, as is evidenced in two ways. First, as the revelation says, "There is never but one on the earth at a time on whom this power and the keys of this priesthood are conferred" (Doctrine and Covenants 132:7). The "keys" are the authority to direct how priesthood power is used and to whom it may be delegated on earth. So great and important are the keys of the sealing power that sometimes we equate the keys of the kingdom with the keys of the sealing power. For example, Jesus said to Peter, the chief Apostle, "And I will give unto thee the keys of the kingdom of heaven: and whatsoever thou shalt bind [seal] on earth shall be bound in heaven: and whatsoever thou shalt loose on earth shall be loosed in heaven" (Matthew 16:19).

Second, the fulness of the priesthood can be exercised and received only in dedicated temples of the Lord. The Prophet Joseph Smith declared, "If a man gets a fulness of the Priesthood of God he has to get it in the same way that Jesus Christ obtained it, and that was by keeping all the commandments and obeying all the ordinances of the house of the Lord."[2]

Commenting on this principle, President Joseph Fielding Smith further stated, "Let me put this in a little different way. I do not care what office you hold in this Church—you may be an apostle, you may be a patriarch, a high priest, or anything else—you cannot receive the fulness of the priesthood unless you go into the temple of the Lord and receive these ordinances of which the Prophet speaks. No [one] can get the fulness of the priesthood outside the temple of the Lord."[3] But the fulness of the priesthood is available to anyone who is worthy to enter the house of the Lord.

Fulness of the Priesthood Anciently

Joseph Smith's statement about how one gets the fulness of the priesthood is intriguing. It implies that Jesus Christ Himself participated in the sealing ordinances. We understand that these ordinances were available in the Church of Jesus Christ of former days. President Heber C. Kimball taught that the temple ordinances performed in The Church of Jesus Christ of Latter-day Saints are principally the same as those that existed in the ancient Church of the meridian dispensation and that Jesus "inducted His apostles into these ordinances."[4] President Joseph Fielding Smith stated that he believed that Peter, James, and John received the sacred endowment on the Mount of Transfiguration.[5]

Peter himself said of their experience on the Mount of Transfiguration, "For we have not followed cunningly devised fables, when we made known unto you the power and coming of our Lord Jesus Christ, but were eyewitnesses of his majesty. For he received from God the Father honour and glory, when there came such a voice to him from the excellent glory, saying, This is my beloved Son, in whom I am well pleased. And this voice which came from heaven we heard, when we were with him in the holy mount. We have also a more sure word of prophecy" (2 Peter 1:16–19). In an 1843 revelation, the Prophet Joseph Smith declared, "The more sure word of prophecy means a man's knowing that he is sealed up unto eternal life, by revelation and the spirit of prophecy through the power of the Holy Ghost" (Doctrine and Covenants 130:5).

Peter, James, and John were blessed by the sealing power of the priesthood. In his second epistle, Peter exhorts other disciples (us) to obtain "godliness" and become "partakers of the divine nature" (2 Peter 1:4). In other words, he urges us to strive to become like God and to "give diligence to make [our] calling and election sure"—a phrase synonymous with being sealed to eternal life. As the Prophet Joseph Smith explained:

> After a person has faith in Christ, repents of his sins, and is baptized for the remission of his sins and receives the Holy Ghost (by the laying on of hands), which is the first Comforter, then let him continue to humble himself, before God, hungering and thirsting after righteousness, and living by every word of God, and the Lord will soon say unto him, Son, thou shalt be exalted. When the Lord has thoroughly proved him, and finds that the man is determined to serve Him at all hazards, then the man will find his calling and election made sure, then it will be his privilege to receive the other Comforter, which the Lord had promised the saints, as is recorded in the testimony of St. John in the 14th chapter, from the 12th to the 27th verses. . . . Now what is this other Comforter? It is no more nor less than the Lord Jesus Christ Himself. . . . And this is the state and place the ancient Saints arrived at when they had such glorious visions—Isaiah, Ezekiel, John upon the Isle of Patmos, St Paul in the three heavens.[6]

Other evidence that the ancient Apostles understood and enjoyed the fulness of the priesthood may be seen in the Apocalypse of John the Revelator, wherein he describes Jesus Christ as "the faithful witness [of God the Father], and the first begotten of the dead, and the prince of the kings of the earth . . . [who] loved us, and washed us from our sins in his own blood, and hath made us kings and priests unto God" (Revelation 1:5–6). As we learn in temples of our day, becoming kings and priests, queens and priestesses, unto God is the ultimate goal and result of receiving the fulness of the priesthood. One cannot become a king or queen, priest or priestess, without the fulness of the priesthood (see Doctrine and Covenants 76:56).

The creation of a kingdom of kings and queens, priests and priestesses, seems to have always been the intention of our Father in Heaven and His Son, Jesus Christ, in every dispensation when the Melchizedek Priesthood has been in operation. When the children of Israel camped at the base of Mount Sinai during their exodus from Egypt, the Lord promised, "If ye will obey my voice indeed, and keep my covenant, then ye shall be a peculiar treasure unto me above all people. . . . And ye shall be unto me a kingdom of priests, and a holy nation" (Exodus 19:5–6). The "priests" spoken of here are not Aaronic or Levitical priests, for the lesser priesthood had not yet been organized. As we are told in modern revelation, Moses plainly taught this glorious possibility to the children of Israel "that they might behold the face of God; But they hardened their hearts and could not endure his presence; therefore, the Lord in his wrath, for his anger was kindled against them, swore that they should not enter into his rest while in the wilderness, which rest is the fulness of his glory. Therefore, he took Moses out of their midst, and the Holy Priesthood also; And the lesser priesthood continued" (Doctrine and Covenants 84:23–26).

Thus, we learn that without the fulness of the priesthood, no one can see the face of God, and no one can enter the fulness of His glory. There is no exaltation in the kingdom of God without the fulness of the priesthood. In our dispensation, the fulness of the priesthood is obtainable only in the house of the Lord. Again, President Joseph Fielding Smith said, "Only in the temple of the Lord can the fulness of the priesthood be received. Now that temples are on the earth, there is no other place where the endowment and the sealing power for all eternity can be given. No man [or woman] can receive the keys of exaltation in any other place."[7] Significantly, those who receive the endowment and sealing ordinances in the Lord's temples today are heirs of a long history and continuity of priesthood operation throughout the dispensations of the gospel on this earth.

Symbolic Gates

In addition, the sealing ordinances of the temple represent a symbolic gate. Just as the ordinance of baptism represents a gate—to the celestial kingdom and to membership in the Savior's earthly Church, The Church of Jesus Christ of Latter-day Saints—so too do the sealing ordinances of the holy priesthood represent a gate that grants admission to the highest degree of the celestial kingdom (see Doctrine and Covenants 131:1–2) and admission to the Savior's heavenly Church—the Church of the Firstborn (see Doctrine and Covenants 76:54). The scriptures describe members of the Church of the Firstborn in the following way:

> They are they into whose hands the Father has given all things—
>
> They are they who are *priests and kings*, who have received of his *fulness*, and of his glory;
>
> And are priests of the Most High, after the order of Melchizedek, which was after the order of Enoch, which was after the order of the Only Begotten Son.
>
> Wherefore, as it is written, they are gods, even the sons of God—
>
> Wherefore, all things are theirs. . . .
>
> And they shall overcome all things. . . .
>
> These are they who have come to an innumerable company of angels, to the general assembly and church of Enoch, and of the Firstborn. . . .
>
> These are they who are just men made perfect through Jesus the mediator of the new covenant, who wrought out this perfect atonement through the shedding of his own blood. (Doctrine and Covenants 76:55–59, 60, 67, 69; emphasis added)

In this passage, we note at least three important principles relating to our present discussion. First, the fulness of God's glory is tied to becoming kings and priests, queens and priestesses, which comes through obtaining the fulness of the priesthood, as earlier described. Second, those who receive a fulness are gods. And third, becoming a member of the Church of the Firstborn is ultimately made possible through the Atonement of Jesus Christ. Our Redeemer is at the core of everything we do. The higher priesthood was originally named for

Him and referred to His power and authority—"the Holy Priesthood, after the Order of the Son of God" (Doctrine and Covenants 107:3). When we are ordained and receive the Melchizedek Priesthood, we "are made like unto the Son of God" (Joseph Smith Translation, Hebrews 7:3 [in Hebrews 7:3, footnote *a*]). It's little wonder then that Jesus Christ is referred to as our "great high priest" (Hebrews 4:14).

Only those who have received the fulness of the priesthood belong to the Church of the Firstborn. Elder Bruce R. McConkie put it this way: "And as *The Church of Jesus Christ* is his earthly church, so the *Church of the Firstborn* is his heavenly church, albeit its members are limited to exalted beings, for whom the family unit continues and who gain an inheritance in the highest heaven of the celestial world."[8] On another occasion, Elder McConkie wrote:

> Members of The Church of Jesus Christ of Latter-day Saints who so devote themselves to righteousness that they receive the higher ordinances of exaltation become members of the Church of the Firstborn. Baptism is the gate to the church itself, but celestial marriage is the gate to membership in the Church of the Firstborn, the inner circle of faithful saints who are heirs of exaltation and the fullness of the Father's kingdom. The Church of the Firstborn is made up of the sons of God, those who have been adopted into the family of the Lord, those who are destined to be joint heirs with Christ in receiving all that the Father hath.[9]

THE HOUSE OF THE LORD

Dedicated temples, or houses of the Lord, are the places where men and women become joint heirs with Jesus Christ. They are places where we are invited in as honored guests of the Lord, literally to His home on earth, where He can reside because of their sanctified environment, as I learned in a stunning way.

Almost ten years after my family and I had been sealed, I found myself back in the Salt Lake Temple as a full-time missionary, preparing to serve the Lord and attending a special session with the other missionaries in our group. We were seated quietly on the fourth floor, waiting for President Harold B. Lee to come and instruct us. As he entered, we stood to honor a senior Apostle, and the Spirit of the

Lord intensified in the large room. The impact was physical as well as spiritual. At a certain point, President Lee invited questions about anything, including questions about the temple and its ordinances. All of us were impressed by President Lee's ability to answer questions straight from the scriptures, which he had with him. When a question would be asked, I remember this spiritual giant would say something like, "Well, let's see what the Lord has to say about the matter." He would then read a passage from the standard works that answered the question.

I don't remember all of the questions, but I do remember one with clarity. President Lee called upon a young elder, probably my age. The elder stood and said, "On the outside of the temple it says this is the house of the Lord. Do you think He has ever been here?" As a nineteen-year-old, overwhelmed by all I had experienced, I thought it was a pretty good question. But then I saw President Lee close his scriptures, put them to the side of the podium, and look at the elder with what I thought was a stern expression, and I began to think maybe President Lee thought the question wasn't so good. As near as I can recollect, President Lee wagged his finger and said, "Oh, elder, do not ask if He has ever been here. This is His house—and He walks these very halls."

It was a dramatic moment; it was as though an electric shock coursed through me. I had never heard anything like that before. President Lee's answer was nothing less than breathtaking. I don't think I heard anything else that transpired in the meeting after that. "He walks these very halls."[10] That statement has shaped my feelings about the temple, about the sealing power, about the fulness of the priesthood, and about the Savior's nearness to us, from that day to this one. I do not take lightly, nor view as metaphor, statements such as the one from President Russell M. Nelson: "A temple is literally the house of the Lord."[11]

Conclusion

When I hear of the Salt Lake Temple, when I see images of it, or when I drive by it, I immediately think of the word *power*—power to change lives, power to alter history, power to bless and sanctify our heavenly parents' children. I also think of the word *security*. I have deep feelings for the Salt Lake Temple. My experiences in that holy house changed my life and my outlook forever. In this, I think there is a possible lesson. I wonder if there would not be significant value in having fathers and mothers spend more time with their children talking about the ordinances of eternity and the sealing power that binds families together forever, and the intimate connection between the power of the priesthood and our Lord Jesus Christ. In this day and age of increased anxiety and insecurity among young people, when social media tries to tell them who they are and what they should embrace, I believe our children and grandchildren would be more secure in their faith, be able to see more clearly the reasons to stay worthy of the temple and the reasons for the ordinances of the only true and living church on the earth, be better prepared to face life's challenges, and be more likely to listen to living prophets with appreciation if they could better comprehend the incomparable value of the keys of the fulness of the priesthood and the sealing power found in the temples of the Lord.

These keys of the kingdom are, in a sense, "on loan" to mortals and will someday be given back to their owner and originator. That is to say, "When the Lord comes to reign personally upon the earth during the millennial era, he will take back the keys. Those who have held them will make an accounting to him of their stewardships at the place called Adam-ondi-Ahman, at which gathering Christ will receive 'dominion, and glory, and a kingdom, that all people, nations, and languages, should serve him' (Daniel 7:13–14). Eventually in the celestial day, 'the keys of the kingdom shall be delivered up again unto the Father' (Inspired Version, Luke 3:8)."[12] In the meantime, may we rejoice over the power God has "loaned" to us until we can become as He is.

Notes

1. Joseph Fielding Smith, *Doctrines of Salvation*, ed. Bruce R. McConkie, 3 vols. (Bookcraft, 1955), 2:174.
2. History, 1838–1856, volume D-1 [1 August 1842–1 July 1843], 1572, josephsmithpapers.org.
3. Joseph Fielding Smith, *Doctrines of Salvation*, 3:131.
4. Heber C. Kimball, in *Journal of Discourses*, 10:240–41.
5. Joseph Fielding Smith, *Doctrines of Salvation*, 2:165.

6. History, 1838–1856, volume C-1 [2 November 1838–31 July 1842], 9 [addenda], josephsmithpapers.org.
7. Joseph Fielding Smith, *Doctrines of Salvation*, 2:174.
8. Bruce R. McConkie, *The Promised Messiah* (Deseret Book, 1978), 47; italics in original.
9. Bruce R. McConkie, *Doctrinal New Testament Commentary*, 3 vols. (Bookcraft, 1973), 3:230–231.
10. The foregoing is a summary of my experience first recounted in Andrew C. Skinner, *Temple Worship: 20 Truths That Will Bless Your Life* (Deseret Book, 2007), 150–53.
11. Russell M. Nelson, "Prepare for Blessings of the Temple," *Ensign*, Mar. 2002, 17.
12. Bruce R. McConkie, *Mormon Doctrine*, 2nd ed. (Bookcraft, 1966), 413.

Christ's Appearance to Lorenzo Snow in the Temple

Susan Easton Black

BURIED DEEP IN THE SEPTEMBER 1933 ISSUE OF THE *IMPROVEMENT Era* is the article "An Experience of My Father's" by LeRoi C. Snow. The article was not mentioned in the table of contents of the *Improvement Era*, suggesting it was unworthy of mention. Yet today that same article is the primary focus of a heated debate over whether Jesus Christ appeared to Lorenzo Snow in the Salt Lake Temple. In the article, the author quotes a story told to him by his niece Allie Snow Young Pond, a granddaughter of President Snow:

> One evening while I was visiting grandpa Snow in his room in the Salt Lake Temple, I remained until the door keepers had gone and the night-watchmen had not yet come in, so grandpa said he would take me to the main front entrance and let me out that way. He got his bunch of keys from his dresser. After we left his room and while we were still in the large corridor leading into the celestial room, I was walking several steps ahead of grandpa when he stopped me and said: "Wait a moment, Allie, I want to tell you something. It was right here that the Lord Jesus Christ appeared to me at the time of the death of President Woodruff. He instructed me to go right ahead and reorganize the First Presidency of the Church at

once and not wait as had been done after the death of the previous presidents, and that I was to succeed President Woodruff."

Then grandpa came a step nearer and held out his left hand and said: "He stood right here, about three feet above the floor. It looked as though He stood on a plate of solid gold."

Grandpa told me what a glorious personage the Savior is and described His hands, feet, countenance, and beautiful white robes, all of which were of such a glory of whiteness and brightness that he could hardly gaze upon Him.

Then he came another step nearer and put his right hand on my head and said: "Now granddaughter, I want you to remember that this is the testimony of your grandfather, that he told you with his own lips that he actually saw the Savior, here in the Temple, and talked with Him face to face."[1]

Since its printing in the *Improvement Era*, the Allie Pond story has been reprinted in the April 2, 1938, *Church News* section of the *Deseret News* as "Remarkable Manifestation to Lorenzo Snow"; in N. B. Lundwall's compilation *Temples of the Most High* (1972), in the *Teaching of Presidents of the Church* series (2012), and in the *Ensign* as "A Visit from the Savior" (September 2015), to name but a few. If there were disbelievers of the account at its first or subsequent printings, they remained silent. In contrast, the faithful spoke of Christ appearing to Lorenzo Snow as one of the signature moments in Church history. In a crowded field of professors, institute and seminary instructors, and Sunday School teachers, I have shared the story, never anticipating that in 2016 an article by John P. Hatch—"From Prayer to Visitation: Reexamining Lorenzo Snow's Vision of Jesus Christ in the Salt Lake Temple" in the *Journal of Mormon History*—would question its truthfulness.[2]

Since then, the veracity of the account of Jesus appearing to Lorenzo Snow and the integrity of Allie Pond, LeRoi C. Snow, and named Church leaders in the article have been questioned. The granddaughter is accused of embellishing and even fabricating the account. The author is accused of grandstanding, and Church leaders are criticized for never writing of the appearance of Christ to President Snow—if, indeed, it did happen. With only a four-paragraph account written thirty-five years after the event, Hatch has concluded that the visitation is suspect and falls into the category of "Mormon myths." The reason behind the conclusion? All accounts of Lorenzo Snow seeing Christ in the temple trace back to Allie Pond and her story, which was printed in an obscure article by her uncle, LeRoi Snow.

No Questions Raised

No questions were raised in Hatch's contentious article about Lorenzo Snow's devotion to temples or temple-building. Historical records reveal that Snow attended meetings in the Kirtland Temple and collected donations to fund the Nauvoo Temple. He spoke at a dedicatory session of the Logan Temple and read the dedicatory prayer in the Manti Temple. On his eightieth birthday, the *Deseret News* printed, "In the evening of his days, [Snow is] still busy and earnest in the great cause to which he has given his earlier years[;] he is continuing within the sacred precincts of the Temple the glorious labors to which he and his associates have consecrated themselves—labors of such profound importance to this sin and death-afflicted world."[3]

As for President Snow's commitment to the Salt Lake Temple, when Church architect Joseph Don Carlos Young learned that President Woodruff wanted the interior of the temple to be completed within a year, Young submitted his resignation. In contrast, Snow accepted an appointment to serve on a temple committee whose purpose was to finish the temple within the year. At the capstone ceremony of the Salt Lake Temple held on April 6, 1892, Snow led about 40,000 Saints in the Hosanna Shout. Exactly one year later, he led those assembled in the Salt Lake Temple in the same shout. Within a month of the temple dedication, Wilford Woodruff named Snow president of the Salt Lake Temple.

Similarly, no "red flags" were raised over LeRoi Snow's recollection of President Woodruff's declining health in 1898 or that doctors despaired for the venerable prophet's life and suggested coastal sea breezes as a remedy. The same goes for LeRoi's account of Lorenzo Snow pleading in the Holy of Holies that the Lord "spare President Woodruff's life [that Woodruff] might outlive him and the great responsibility of Church leadership would not fall upon his shoulders."[4] Likewise, the account of President Woodruff dying on Friday, September 2, 1898, at the Victorian-style home of Isaac Trumbo was accepted, as was the telegram announcing his death being wired to the President's Office in Salt Lake City and forwarded to Lorenzo Snow, who was visiting family in Brigham City. No questions were raised about Snow sending a telegram announcing his departure from Brigham City on the 5:40 p.m. train. Likewise, there were no hints of disagreement over his reaching the city and being conveyed to the Salt Lake Temple where he again entered the Holy of Holies to commune with God.

Surprisingly, Hatch's article missed quoting from Lorenzo Snow's October 1897 general conference address: "There is no man that knows the truth of this work more than I do. I know it fully; I know it distinctly. I know there is a God just as well as any man knows it, because God has revealed himself to me. I know it positively. I shall never forget the manifestations of the Lord; I never will forget them as long as memory endures. It is in me."[5]

But not wishing to contend that at this and other times President Snow spoke of the Lord revealing Himself to him, it is safe to say that the only issue raised in the Hatch article is whether Lorenzo Snow was visited by Jesus Christ in the Salt Lake Temple between the death of Wilford Woodruff and the sustaining of Snow as Church President. As to that question, the Hatch article presents an earlier account of the Allie Pond story given by LeRoi Snow at the June 8, 1919, M.I.A. officers meeting held in the Assembly Hall.[6] Unfortunately, apart from naming the hymns sung and reporting that "a number of very impressive testimonies were born [sic] by different speakers," Church leaders did not take official minutes.[7] Only the words of LeRoi reveal that "President Heber J. Grant immediately arose in confirmation of the testimony given by Brother LeRoi C. Snow quoting the grand-daughter of Lorenzo Snow."[8]

With that admission, we have the first Church leader verifying the account. During President Grant's remaining years in the First Presidency, he had hundreds of occasions to speak at small and large gatherings. Never once did he take the opportunity to negate the account of Christ's appearance to Lorenzo Snow even though he was well aware that the story had gained traction in Church circles and was repeated often.

Then there was Anthon H. Lund, serving in the First Presidency with Heber J. Grant at the time of the June 1919 M.I.A. conference. In his September 1933 article, LeRoi wrote, "A few days after the M.I.A. conference, in an interview with President [Anthon H.] Lund in his office . . . he said that he heard father tell a number of times of the Savior's appearance to him after he had dressed in his temple robes, presented himself before the Lord and offered up the signs of the Priesthood."[9] Unfortunately, President Lund died in 1921. In the two-year gap between the M.I.A. conference and his death, Lund had many occasions to speak to audiences both large and small. On those occasions, he never refuted the statement.

Myth or Truth?

Although the Hatch article states that the search for other accounts of the story has proven fruitless, there is a glaring error in his assumption that the appearance of Jesus Christ to Lorenzo Snow is a "Mormon myth." The error is in not acknowledging the character or Church position of those who knew of the account.

Allie Snow Young Pond

The earliest known account of Allie being in the Salt Lake Temple was when she sang in the choir at the dedication. Following the dedication, she was endowed and sealed to her husband, Noah S. Pond (1872–1955), in the Salt Lake Temple. Lorenzo Snow officiated at the sealing.

Next follows her account of Jesus Christ appearing to President Snow. At the time, Allie was a young mother in her early twenties living in Salt Lake City with her parents and caring for her one-year-old son. Her husband was serving a Scandinavian mission. After he completed an honorable mission, he and Allie moved to Pocatello, Idaho. In that small agrarian community, Allie took an active role in Primary, Y.W.M.I.A., and the Relief Society. For several years, she was president of the Mother's Class in the Relief Society. When Noah Pond served as president of the Northern States Mission (1898–1900), Allie served as president of the Relief Society of the Northern States Mission.

Allie lived ten years beyond the publication of the 1933 *Improvement Era* article. Being active in the auxiliaries of the Church, she had a forum in which to recant her story or question her memory of speaking with Grandpa Snow in the Salt Lake Temple. She never did so. It is significant that three years after Allie's death, at the behest of the Twelve, Elder John A. Widtsoe inquired about the story to Noah Pond. In his correspondence on October 30, 1946, Elder Widtsoe did not question the veracity of the account. He wrote instead, "We all know from unquestioned evidence that President Snow had a deivine [sic] manifestation in the temple."[10] Noah Pond responded to Elder Widtsoe on November 12, 1946: "Frequently before Allie's death, we talked about the great privilege that was hers in visiting grandfather, President Lorenzo Snow, in the Salt Lake Temple on the memorable evening of his narrative of the Heavenly visitation of the Savior to him and the instructions given him to proceed forthwith in the reorganization of the First Presidency of the Church. . . . President Snow's statement was very definite that he saw the Savior and heard his voice. Allie promptly related the incident to her parents."[11]

Brother Pond then wrote, "The facts as given by Brother LeRoi C. Snow . . . [were] readily confirmed by the testimoney [sic] of President Grant who was of course present when [the account of] the Savior's visit was given by President Snow to the First Presidency and the Council of Apostles."[12]

LeRoi Clarence Snow

After his father, Lorenzo Snow, was called to be president of the Salt Lake Temple in May 1893, LeRoi was appointed librarian of the temple. He served in that position until receiving a proselyting mission call to Germany in 1896. On his mission, LeRoi presided over the Munich Bavaria Branch and the Dresden Conference. Returning to Salt Lake City, he served as his father's private secretary and as a member of the general board of the Y.M.M.I.A. He later served as an assistant Church historian. From 1922 to 1924 he served in the Eastern States Mission. Upon returning to Utah, LeRoi was named the first president of the Salt Lake Mission Home (1924–1928).

Living twenty-nine years after writing his September 1933 article, LeRoi had many occasions to break from the Allie Pond story, but he did not. Can we conceive that such a man would let a fabricated story gain traction?

ARTHUR WINTER

In his September 1933 article, LeRoi Snow wrote, "After the [Eighteenth Ward sacrament] meeting Elder Arthur Winter told me he also had heard my father tell of the Savior's appearance to him in the Temple."[13] Arthur served as the official stenographer of the Church. In 1897 he helped President Woodruff record his testimony into a "talking machine." Arthur was with Lorenzo Snow when Snow gave his now-famous talk on tithing in the St. George Tabernacle. Upon learning of Arthur's death, President Heber J. Grant had the flag atop the Church offices lowered to half-mast in his honor. Could such a man want to deceive LeRoi Snow by telling him that his father saw Christ in the temple?

CONCLUSION

What good comes from questioning the account of Lorenzo Snow seeing Jesus Christ in the temple? The question sullies the reputations of Allie Pond, LeRoi Snow, Arthur Winters, and Presidents Heber J. Grant and Anthon H. Lund. What the Hatch article fails to recognize is the sterling character and longevity of those named in the *Improvement Era* article and the fact that each had opportunities to retract their statements as printed but did not. Although it is true that documents have not surfaced to verify the Allie Pond story, let us not shut the door to the possibility that documents will yet emerge. In the meantime, I am satisfied that this signature Church account will continue to inspire Latter-day Saints throughout the world.

NOTES

1. LeRoi C. Snow, "An Experience of My Father's," *Improvement Era*, Sept. 1933, 677.
2. John P. Hatch, "From Prayer to Visitation: Reexamining Lorenzo Snow's Vision of Jesus Christ in the Salt Lake Temple," *Journal of Mormon History* 42, no. 3 (July 2016): 155–82.
3. *Deseret Evening News*, Apr. 3, 1894, quoted in *Teachings of Presidents of the Church: Lorenzo Snow* (2012), 25.
4. Snow, "Experience of My Father's," 677.

5. Lorenzo Snow, in Conference Report, Oct. 1897, 32.
6. The annual M.I.A. meeting was typically held in April in conjunction with general conference, but as soldiers returned to their homes following the Armistice of November 1918, there was a resurgence of the deadly influenza. In the greater Salt Lake area, quarantine signs were placed on homes where victims had contracted influenza. With 2,000 quarantine signs still up in April 1919, the general conference and the M.I.A. conference were delayed until June. See Trent Toone, "Looking Back at General Conference in the Age of Influenza Outbreaks and World War I," *Church News*, Apr. 6, 2019.
7. Hatch, "From Prayer to Visitation," 170.
8. Snow, "Experience of My Father's," 677.
9. Snow, "Experience of My Father's," 679.
10. Elder John A. Widtsoe to Noah Pond, October 30, 1946, Church History Library, Salt Lake City.
11. Noah Pond to Elder John A. Widtsoe, November 12, 1946, Church History Library, Salt Lake City.
12. Pond to Widtsoe, November 12, 1946.
13. Snow, "Experience of My Father's," 679.

Part 3

Patrons' Personal Experiences in the Salt Lake Temple

Baby Born in the Salt Lake Temple

Chad S. Hawkins & Katie Lambert[1]

THE SALT LAKE TEMPLE'S DEDICATION TRANSPIRED OVER MULTIPLE days during the month of April in 1893. On the temple's second day of services, a truly unique experience occurred. Emma Bennett from Provo, Utah, gave birth to a son *in* the temple at the close of the day's many events. Sister Bennett, who had been attending the dedication session in the temple's assembly room, suddenly began to have labor pains.

Elder James E. Talmage noted the event in his diary: "A Sister Bennett from Provo was taken with labor pains and gave easy birth to a son. She was moved from the Assembly Room to a small apartment [in the temple]. Some sects would hold that such an event desecrated the holy place; but the Latter-day Saints will take a directly opposite view." The baby was born around 10:00 p.m.

Eight days later, on April 15, Emma and her husband, Benjamin, who had been staying nearby, returned to the temple with their newborn son to receive a special blessing in the room in which he was born. In the blessing, Joseph F. Smith named the baby boy Joseph Temple Bennett.

Notes

1. Reprint: Previously published in Chad S. Hawkins and Katie Lambert, "Unbelievable Stories of Babies Born in Latter-day Saint Temples," *LDS Living*, June 26, 2017, https://www.ldsliving.com/4-unbelievable-stories-of-babies-born-in-lds-temples/s/81801.

"All Will Be Well Because of Temple Covenants"

President Henry B. Eyring[1]

I HAVE BEEN BLESSED TO FEEL . . . PEACE EVERY TIME I ENTER THE sacred temple. I recall the first day I walked into the Salt Lake Temple. I was a young man.

I looked up at a high white ceiling that made the room so light it seemed almost as if it were open to the sky. And in that moment, the thought came into my mind in clear words: "I have been in this lighted place before." But then immediately there came into my mind, not in my own voice, these words: "No, you have never been here before. You are remembering a moment before you were born. You were in a sacred place like this where the Lord could come."

Brothers and sisters, I humbly testify that as we attend the temple, we can be reminded of the eternal nature of our spirits, our relationship with the Father and His divine Son, and our ultimate desire to return to our heavenly home.

Notes

1. Reprint: Previously published in Henry B. Eyring, "All Will Be Well Because of Temple Covenants," *Liahona*, May 2014, 24–27.

Testimony-Building Experiences in the Salt Lake Temple

Craig James Ostler

I HAVE SEVERAL SPECIAL PERSONAL CONNECTIONS WITH THE HISTORic temple in Salt Lake City. I was born in Salt Lake County and lived there until I left for college and to serve a full-time mission. During those years, the Salt Lake Temple was the only temple in the Salt Lake Valley. All of my Primary, Sunday School, and Aaronic Priesthood classes displayed photographs of the Salt Lake Temple during lessons regarding temple ordinances. Thus, it should be no surprise that any of my thoughts or goals to someday receive temple ordinances focused on the Salt Lake Temple.

Later, when I attended seminary classes, it was not unusual to have displays or bulletin boards highlighting temples. I learned of the then additional twelve dedicated and operating temples, most of which were up and down the Rocky Mountain corridor where the main membership of the Church lived. Nevertheless, they were located in places that seemed very distant from my life. Shopping trips as a youth and later excursions to downtown Salt Lake City as a teenager led us right to the area of Temple Square. Whether consciously or subconsciously, the reminder of a future day when I would someday enter that marvelous and somewhat mysterious sacred building accompanied each of those visits to Salt Lake City.

Even in our home, I had regular reminders of the Salt Lake Temple. As a young man, my father had cards printed with his name and address to be given to others while he served a full-time mission. The background of these cards showed Temple Square with the Salt Lake Temple as the main focus and the thirteen Articles of Faith printed on the reverse side. The Korean War interrupted his mission service. Between the time he spent in the Salt Lake City Mission Home and when he was given his train ticket to the Central States Mission, he received orders from the draft board requiring him to immediately report to the United States Air Force. My parents married soon after the Korean conflict reached a resolution. Consequently, my father did not serve a mission and had hundreds of these unused personalized cards in our home. He gave me free access to carry the cards with me and to gaze upon them whenever I desired.

I connected the Salt Lake Temple with the teachings declared in the Articles of Faith—that the temple and the principles of the Restoration of the gospel were one whole. Possibly an even more important personal connection to this house of the Lord while in my youth is that when my parents married, they were sealed in the Salt Lake Temple, and any time thereafter that they participated in temple ordinances while I lived in their home, it was within that temple. I watched as they laid the sacred temple clothing out on their bed in preparation for attending the temple. In my mind, I tried to associate that clothing with the temple that I had seen so often and looked forward to the time when I could also do as they were doing.

Ancestral Connection

My connection to the Salt Lake Temple goes back several generations. According to our family history, my third-great-grandfather, James Morris Farmer, worked on the Salt Lake Temple as a stonemason. When the original foundation of the temple was found to be unstable and needed to be strengthened, Brigham Young appointed James Farmer as a foreman on Temple Square. He, along with others, taught men how to cut the granite blocks for the foundation from the gigantic boulders brought from Little Cottonwood Canyon. I believe that this connection, as well as the many family members who were endowed and sealed there, are additional reasons why my family felt that the Salt Lake Temple was their temple.

Endowment and the Assembly Hall

A red-letter, five-star day in my life will always be March 8, 1973. That was the day I received my endowment in the Salt Lake Temple. Unfortunately, my parents did not have temple recommends at that time. One of my roommates at Brigham Young University, Gaylin Sharp, learned that I was going to the temple alone and quickly volunteered to be my escort for that special evening. Gaylin was a returned missionary and four years older than I was. I believe that much of the peace, comfort, and confidence I felt in an unfamiliar situation was due to his gentle spirit and love.

We sat together in the front row of each of the endowment rooms as we moved from location to location. Photographs that I had seen of the interior of the temple came to life as I made sacred covenants, received signs and tokens, and was filled with awe and wonder at the grandeur of the endowment presentation. The endowment was presented by live individuals rather than the films that were used in most temples that followed. I believe that the live nature of the presentation made it even more meaningful and personal. Most importantly, wearing the temple garment for the first time and dressed in the robes of the priesthood while sitting in the celestial room, I felt like a royal son of Deity prepared to do all that my Father in Heaven expected of me.

It makes me feel like I am ancient history to have been one of the many individuals who went to the Mission Home in Salt Lake City before going either to a Language Training Mission or directly into the mission field. But such was the blessing that I received. This occasion provided another important experience with the Salt Lake Temple. Many of the elders and sisters who reported as missionaries to the Salt Lake Mission Home did not have temples near their family homes. Consequently, they had not received their endowment. On our third day in the Mission Home (Monday, June 18, 1973), we fasted because we were going to the Salt Lake Temple, joining those who were receiving the endowment at that time.

We had the blessing of participating in two endowment sessions. I had the privilege of attending many temple endowment sessions since first receiving my endowment, and I had a sharp recall of the words in the presentation. While somewhat embarrassing for me to admit today, I noted with some smugness that a few of those participating in the live presentation of the endowment that day erred in the appropriate and approved dialogue. I later felt very repentant when, having prideful thoughts at having judged their errors, a powerful story was shared. I have tried to find the story in publications, but I have not yet been successful. Nevertheless, the principle shared in the story is a powerful one for me.

Apparently, during one of the endowment presentations in the Salt Lake Temple, which included General Authorities as participants, errors were made by one of the nervous presenters. Following the endowment session, the group met together for a meeting and to receive some instruction. A member of the First Presidency referred to the errors of the nervous presenter in the temple endowment. He articulated an important thought to consider. He related that many gathered in that meeting may have noticed the errors in the individual's wording. However, he declared, the individual who was doing his best and made those errors was not being tested. Rather, the participants were the ones being tested as to their grace for him. This principle cut deep into my prideful heart, and I have sought to give greater grace to others in their errors ever since. I have thought of this lesson from my experience in the Salt Lake Temple when I have participated in live presentations of the endowment and other temple ordinances or as adjustments have been made to the temple ordinances.

After the two endowment sessions, I, along with the other missionaries, climbed the stairs to the Assembly Hall, which occupies the entire upper floor of the Salt Lake Temple. President Harold B. Lee regularly met with missionaries in the Salt Lake Mission Home following the scheduled endowment sessions. He gave some brief remarks regarding temple ordinances and then opened the remaining time to questions we might have regarding those ordinances. I am still amazed that I had the tenacity and youthful arrogance to ask President Lee a question regarding a specific aspect of the endowment presentation. As President Lee answered my question and the questions of the other missionaries, I noticed that he patiently turned to passages in his opened scriptures that perfectly addressed those questions. This experience provided another impressive and important lesson that I received in the Salt Lake Temple and that I have tried to follow all my life—that is, when answering gospel questions, turn to the answers the Lord has given in the standard works rather than sharing my own best thinking.

I had the opportunity to return to the Assembly Hall of the Salt Lake Temple for an important meeting with the President of the Church one other time. In 1996 President Gordon B. Hinckley invited bishops and stake presidents from various regions to meet together in the Salt Lake Temple. At that time, I was serving as a bishop of a BYU married-student ward and thus received an invitation to one such meeting held on Sunday, December 16 of that year. A BYU faculty colleague and good friend, Guy Dorius, was also serving as a bishop in the same BYU stake. The two of us, along with our homeward bishop, Paul Burgon, determined to travel together from our homes in Pleasant Grove, Utah, to the Salt Lake Temple. The meeting was scheduled to begin at 10 a.m., and we were asked to arrive by 9 a.m. in the parking area beneath the Church Office Building plaza. We thought that it would be an even better idea to arrive earlier, by 8 a.m. To our amazement, it appeared that most everyone else who had been invited had the same idea. We all lined up near the doors that led to the underground tunnel that would take us to the temple.

Those doors soon opened, and we were escorted with the other bishops and stake presidents to the assembly room. This time I was much more aware of my surroundings than I had been as a young missionary. I took special note of the four tiers of pulpits on each end of the room, similar to those on the two floors of the house of the Lord in Kirtland, Ohio, and later in Nauvoo. We were seated in folding chairs that were placed on the main floor, while others were seated in the balcony areas on each side. We sat quietly contemplating what we were experiencing and what the purpose of the meeting might be. A little before 9 a.m., President Hinckley, along with his two counselors in the First Presidency and members of the Quorum of the Twelve Apostles, took their places in the Melchizedek Priesthood pulpits.

To our surprise, President Hinckley did not wait to begin the meeting at the appointed 10 a.m. hour. He announced that he believed that everyone who wished to attend was already seated and that he could see no reason to wait. This was the first, and so far the only, Church meeting I have ever attended that began an hour early! Following the opening hymn and prayer, President Hinckley announced that the main reason for our meeting was to partake of the emblems of the sacrament together.

Elders Neal A. Maxwell and David B. Haight administered the sacramental prayers, Elder Maxwell offering the prayer on the bread and Elder Haight on the water. I recall this particular detail because, at the time, Elder Haight was blind and offered the prayer from memory. In doing so, he made an error in the revealed wording of the prayer. I am confident that I was not the only one in the meeting to notice because as bishops, we were responsible for presiding over the blessing of the sacramental emblems in our individual wards, which included ensuring that the wording of the prayers was exact. Somewhat to my amazement, President Hinckley did not correct Elder Haight or ask him to offer the prayer a second time. I thought then and have since of the lesson taught earlier regarding grace for others' errors in a moment of sincerity, especially in the temple.

After the blessing of the bread and water, members of the Quorum of the Twelve Apostles passed the sacrament to those assembled. I felt like I needed to pinch myself when Elder Boyd K. Packer passed the sacrament to me. I experienced a love for and unity with the presiding authorities of the Church as well as the other bishops and stake presidents. I wondered if the spirit of that meeting might be similar to what the people in the Book of Mormon experienced when the Savior administered and partook of the sacrament with them (see 3 Nephi 18:11). This occasion changed how I partake of the sacramental emblems, giving greater emphasis that I am witnessing unto the Father that I remember His Son. In addition, this experience caused me to look forward with greater hope that I might be present when the Savior returns to partake of the sacrament with past prophets and apostles "and also with all those whom [the] Father hath given [Him] out of the world" (Doctrine and Covenants 27:14; see also Doctrine and Covenants 27:1–14). I believe that the experience of that morning in the Salt Lake Temple is a type of the promised future sacrament meetings that will be held, with the Savior presiding and partaking with those who are present.

It may be of passing interest that President Hinckley did address us on important topics that morning. However, he emphasized that one of the reasons he wished to meet with us in the Salt Lake Temple was to speak to us in the privacy of the temple. He emphasized that he hoped he wouldn't read in the papers the next day quotes and misquotes of what he had said. He asked us to keep private his teachings that day but to live by the principles he shared and use them to guide those we presided over.

"I Wondered If I Would Ever Enter"

My late brother-in-law, Ralph Owen, taught me a lesson about the symbolic power of the Salt Lake Temple. Ralph, my wife's oldest brother, sat with me outside the Salt Lake Temple on the day he was married and sealed.

Ralph had grown up in Portland, Oregon. His mother had many relatives in the Salt Lake City area, and when he was young, his family made regular trips to visit them. Often, they would also visit Temple Square, where Ralph would gaze up at what to him was a mysterious building: the Salt Lake Temple. It was mysterious because he could only imagine what occurred inside it. He desired to enter the temple someday and learn for himself what it meant to enter into temple covenants.

Ralph had made early choices in life that prevented him from entering the house of the Lord until he was over fifty years old. As we visited on this special day in his life, he continued to fix his gaze on the magnificent historic Salt Lake Temple while he shared his feelings. He confessed to me in words along these lines: "When I was younger, I came here so many times. I sat with my dad like you and I are doing, and he taught me how important this building is. Through the years, I wondered if I would ever enter the doors of this temple. As the years passed, I believed that it became less and less likely that that dream would be fulfilled, but I always carried the hope in my heart that someday . . ." His voice faltered and tears filled his eyes, all while he continued to look upon the outside walls of the temple. This structure had become a symbol of hope and longing to be worthy to enter the house of the Lord. For Ralph, entering the Salt Lake Temple was the fulfillment of his youthful goals and hopes. In addition, it was a message to his deceased father that his chair at the family table was not empty. He exclaimed as if his father were present, "Dad, see—I'm making it! I didn't let you down."

Years later, when Ralph's physical and mental health failed him, I returned to Temple Square with him. In early May 2015, his children had transported him from Washington to Utah to attend his mother's funeral. The next day was Sunday, and I encouraged his children, none of whom were active Church members, to take him to see the Salt Lake Temple again. At that time, Ralph was not able to communicate very clearly, but it was evident that he was pleased to be there. I asked for permission to push him in his wheelchair, just the two of us alone, where we could visit for a few minutes. I thought back to the day of his marriage sealing when we sat together and he shared his thoughts about the Salt Lake Temple. I recounted that conversation to him as we moved around the temple grounds. The two of us shared one last connection by contemplating mortality and eternity while focusing on this sacred and historic temple.

The Savior's Visit to President Lorenzo Snow

For many years, I had been familiar with the account of the Savior appearing in the Salt Lake Temple to President Lorenzo Snow, as shared earlier in this compilation. While attending that temple, I wondered where this appearance might have occurred. I had envisioned in my mind the details of the surroundings of this glorious visitation. On one occasion, while in the celestial room, the doors of the Holy of Holies were open. I knew that President Snow had been fervently praying for guidance in this most sacred of temple rooms, after which he left in great disappointment when no answer came. I read of how he passed "through the Celestial room and out into the large corridor."[1] I looked around but could not determine which part of the temple this account referred to.

Later, toward the end of my career at BYU, we met as Religion Department faculty and spouses for an endowment session in the Salt Lake Temple. After leaving the celestial room, a few of us were kindly invited to the aforementioned large corridor and shown where the Savior appeared and spoke face-to-face with President Snow. I had stood and even knelt in other sacred locations near where the Savior had visited as a premortal spirit, in mortality, and following His Resurrection. But there was something different about this exact location that was so very personally intimate. The corridor did not appear to me to be large at all but a small, humble, sacred abode in the Lord's own house. As others left, I found myself unwilling to move. I wanted to hold my sweetheart's hand and contemplate a bit longer the wonder of it all. This hallowed building stands as a witness to the world of many truths of the gospel of Jesus Christ, offering salvation and exaltation for both the living and the dead. For me, its rooms, and even corridors, testify that Jesus Christ is not an absentee Master but personally guides and directs His Church through prophets that He has appointed in these latter days.

Thank you for letting me share a few of my connections and experiences with the Salt Lake Temple. I hope that you appreciate and understand a bit better the significance of this particular temple among others that have been built and are now being built across the earth. For me, "my" temples will always be the Salt Lake Temple and the temple I live the closest to. This may also be the case for you, as the Salt Lake Temple stands as a recognized symbol of the headquarters of The Church of Jesus Christ of Latter-day Saints.

Notes

1. LeRoi C. Snow, "An Experience of My Father's," *Improvement Era,* Sept. 1933, 677.

Great-Grandma Allen's Temple Recommend

Kenneth L. Alford

A TAN, SEVENTY-FIVE-YEAR-OLD PIECE OF CARDSTOCK GIVES ME COMfort whenever I look at it. It's small—just four inches wide and two and a half inches tall. It belonged to one of my paternal great-grandmothers, Mary Gabriella Henderson Allen.

Great-Grandma Allen was the only one of my eight great-grandparents who I ever met, and I have only one recollection of her. The memory is from the summer of 1958, shortly after my father separated from active-duty military service in the US Air Force. After leaving his duty assignment at Fairbanks, Alaska, my father moved our growing family to Ogden, Utah, where he was born and raised. My parents bought a small brick home in a new housing division in the northeast corner of the city, and my father wanted to show it to his Grandma Allen, who was eighty-five years old. I remember she had beautiful white hair and was very soft-spoken. She died in August, just a few weeks later.

It is easy for me to connect to important periods in Church history by considering my great-grandma's life and family. In the spring of 1849, her Henderson grandparents, Robert and Mary Ross, joined the Church in a small village called Penston in East Lothian, Scotland, near the Firth of Forth, and emigrated to northern Utah in 1863.[1] Her father, William Henderson, was a polygamist and served time in a federal penitentiary in Utah before being called by a prophet of God to serve as a full-time missionary in Scotland for several years. Mary was born in Logan, Utah, in March 1873—the first generation in her family to be born in the United States. She was twenty years old when the Salt Lake Temple was dedicated and was newly married when Utah received statehood. Great-Grandma Allen and her family were faithful and active Latter-day Saints throughout their lives.

So what is that small old card of my great-grandma's that I have in my possession? It is a Salt Lake Temple recommend. Unlike temple recommends issued today, that recommend was issued by a specific temple. There are no bishopric or stake presidency signatures. The only signatures on it are hers and the temple president's.

The text printed on the card is straightforward. The preprinted signature of Stephen L. Chipman, who served as the fifth president of the Salt Lake Temple (from 1938 to 1945), appears in the bottom right corner. The back of the recommend is blank. As this temple recommend was issued during the Great Depression, "1940" is stamped in red ink to the left of 1939, showing that her recommend remained valid for an additional year.

My father gave me his grandmother's temple recommend a few months before his death in October 2023. I especially appreciate the fact that it is a Salt Lake Temple recommend—the temple where my paternal grandparents (sealed in July 1935, after having been married civilly in 1919), my parents (married in September 1953), my sweetheart and I (married in April 1979), and one of my children and his bride (married in December 2010) were sealed for time and for all eternity.

Great-Grandma Allen's Salt Lake Temple recommend serves as a wonderful reminder to me of two temple-related principles. First, it reminds me of the importance of living a temple-worthy life. President Howard W. Hunter taught that "the things that we must do and not do to be worthy of a temple recommend are the very things that ensure we will be happy as individuals and as families."[2] He noted that "the Lord desires that His people be a temple-motivated people. It would be the deepest desire of my heart to have every member of the Church be temple worthy. I would hope that every adult member would be worthy of—and carry—a current temple recommend, even if proximity to a temple does not allow immediate or frequent use of it. Let us be a temple-attending and a temple-loving people."[3]

In the concluding chapter of the Book of Mormon, Moroni shares some excellent counsel regarding the importance of being perfected in Christ, or living a temple-worthy life: "Yea, come unto Christ, and be perfected in him, and deny yourselves of all ungodliness; and if ye shall deny yourselves of all ungodliness, and love God with all your might, mind and strength, then is his grace sufficient for you. . . . And again, if ye by the grace of God are perfect in Christ, and deny not his power, then are ye sanctified in Christ by the grace of God, through the shedding of the blood of Christ . . . that ye become holy, without spot" (Moroni 10:32–33).

Keeping ourselves temple worthy demonstrates our love for God, shows an appreciation for the Restoration of the gospel, and blesses our life and the lives of our family members, both in mortality and in the eternities.

Second, Great-Grandma Allen's Salt Lake Temple recommend reminds me of the importance of remaining active and faithful. It takes just one generation to break the chain of generational gospel faithfulness. Speaking to religious educators at a Church-sponsored conference in 2001, Elder Henry B. Eyring commented on this important concept: "The Church has always been one generation away from extinction. If a whole generation were lost, which will not happen, we would lose the Church. But even a single individual lost to the gospel of Jesus Christ closes doors for generations of descendants, unless the Lord reaches out to bring some of them back."[4]

My family history illustrates how quickly the chain of gospel living can be broken. Following some adversity in their lives, two extended family members chose to take a break from the Church for several years. They have subsequently returned to Church activity, but they are now witnessing several generations of their children and grandchildren who remain outside of Church membership, the blessings of activity, and a covenant relationship with our Savior. Elder M. Russell Ballard wisely taught that "the decision to 'walk no more' with Church members and the Lord's chosen leaders will have a long-term impact that cannot always be seen right now."[5] It can be beneficial to consider that "you know there is a plan for us in this life. You know that families can be eternal. Why put yours at risk? Don't be the weak link in this beautiful chain of faith you started, or you received, as a legacy. Be the strong one. It is your turn to do it, and the Lord can help you."[6]

In short, as President Howard W. Hunter encouraged us, we should make "the temple the great symbol" of our Church membership.[7] "If we can pattern our life after the Master, and take his teachings and example as the supreme pattern for our own, we will not find it difficult to be consistent and loyal in every walk of life, for we will be committed to a single, sacred standard of conduct and belief."[8] This is truly the Lord's work, and "He has given it to us. It is our responsibility, our pleasure, and our privilege to carry this work forward."[9] I am grateful that Great-Grandma Allen's Salt Lake Temple recommend has survived the passage of time. It stands as a silent but gentle witness of her commitment and dedication to the gospel of Jesus Christ and invites me to do the same.

Notes

1. For Robert and Mary Henderson's story, see Kenneth L. Alford, "Robert and Mary Henderson," in *Signs, Wonders, and Miracles: Extraordinary Stories from Early Latter-day Saints*, ed. Glenn Rawson and Dennis Lyman (Covenant Communications, 2015), 195–97.
2. Howard W. Hunter, "'Be Partakers of Divine Nature,' Prophet Counsels," *Church News*, Oct. 8, 1994, 6.

3. Howard W. Hunter, "The Great Symbol of Our Membership," *Ensign*, Oct. 1994, 5.
4. Henry B. Eyring, "We Must Raise Our Sights" (address to religious educators at a conference on the Book of Mormon, Brigham Young University, Aug. 14, 2001).
5. M. Russell Ballard, "To Whom Shall We Go?," *Ensign* or *Liahona*, Nov. 2016, 91.
6. Carlos A. Godoy, "For the Sake of Your Posterity," *Liahona*, Nov. 2023, 18.
7. Howard W. Hunter, "The Great Symbol of Our Membership," 2.
8. Howard W. Hunter, "Standing as Witnesses of God," *Ensign*, May 1990, 60.
9. Spencer W. Kimball, "The Things of Eternity—Stand We in Jeopardy?," *Ensign*, Jan. 1977, 7.

The Salt Lake Temple: Home

Derek R. Sainsbury

For me, the Salt Lake Temple feels like home—an eternal home. During these years of its renovation, I have missed it more than I expected. Sure, I feel my heavenly home in other temples, be they in Taylorsville, Utah, where I grew up; in Rome, Italy, the nation in which I served as a missionary; or in Bountiful, Utah, where I currently live. For me, however, there is something distinctly different about the feeling of the Salt Lake Temple, and I have missed it. These words from its original dedicatory prayer come to mind:

> *When the children of Thy people, in years to come, shall be separated, through any cause, from this place,* and their hearts shall turn in remembrance of Thy promises to this holy Temple, and they shall cry unto Thee from the depths of their affliction and sorrow to extend relief and deliverance to them, we humbly entreat Thee to Turn Thine ear in mercy to them; *hearken to their cries, and grant unto them the blessings for which they ask.*"[1]

Why does the Salt Lake Temple hold such power over my heart? Could it be because my great-grandfather, George A. Sainsbury, was one of the original photographers of the temple's exterior and interior? Perhaps it's because of its history or its historic place in ancient prophecy. Maybe it's because that is where Christ's prophets and apostles convene to commune with heaven to lead the kingdom of God and where some have testified of Christ's physical appearance. Or perhaps it is the formidable, fortress-like architecture that has fascinated and inspired me since I was a child. While these reasons are all true, ultimately my love for the Salt Lake Temple comes from the personal experiences I have had inside its granite walls that fulfill the promised blessings offered in its 1893 dedicatory prayer.

Salt Lake Temple capstone ceremony, April 6, 1892. Taken by George A. Sainsbury, great-grandfather of the author.

I was nineteen when I entered the Salt Lake Temple to receive my endowment in preparation for my mission. Admittedly, I was not very well prepared. My parents did not attend the temple often before or after their divorce when I was twelve. No one taught me anything about my upcoming experience. In fact, my temple preparation course was merely a high councilor instructing me how to properly destroy my garments after they were worn out. I was caught completely off guard by the ceremonial clothing and elaborate rituals. It was unlike anything I had experienced in the Church. Yet as I think back, my lack of preparation was a blessing because I entered the house of the Lord more with the mindset of an innocent, curious child.

> "That Thy glory may rest upon it; that Thy holy presence may be continually in it . . . we pray Thee that all people who may enter upon the threshold of this, Thine house, *may feel Thy power and be constrained to acknowledge that Thou hast sanctified it,* that it is Thy house, a place of Thy holiness."[2]

When I entered the temple, I was immediately enveloped in a feeling of the Spirit that I had not experienced before. It was intense, comforting, uplifting, holy, and empowering. I knew that I was on sacred ground. Even the very air I was breathing seemed different. The promised blessings of the initiatory ordinances amazed me. They seemed impossible for someone with my humble and difficult upbringing yet somehow rang true to my heart. As we progressed through the endowment ceremony, I marveled continually at the beauty surrounding me. Intricately painted murals on the walls of the creation, garden, and telestial rooms refocused my mind from the things I did not understand to the beauty and magnificence of God and His love and plan for me. Ascending from room to room, I could feel myself approaching heaven.

All throughout my experience, my heart rehearsed a story that a seminary teacher had shared about the Salt Lake Temple. Missionaries would ask President Harold B. Lee, when he would take them on a tour through the temple, to show them the location where the Savior appeared to Lorenzo Snow, and President Lee's response was that the temple was the Lord's house and that He walked those halls.[3] That was the distinct feeling I had and still remember. I sincerely believed I could turn the next corner or enter the next room and He would be there! This amazing feeling climaxed as I entered the celestial room. I did not see Him; however, I felt Him! Standing in that tall, beautifully ornate room, staring at its magnificent chandelier, I was immersed in heaven. I embraced my mother and grandparents and felt deep within me something I have felt every time since: "*This* is my home."

> "That it may be the *abode of Thy Well-Beloved Son, our Savior*; that the angels who stand before Thy face may be the hallowed messengers who shall visit it, bearing to us Thy wishes and Thy will."[4]

When it was time to leave, I walked down the hall toward the grand staircase. An elderly temple worker, noticing it was my first time in the temple, stopped me and showed me the place where the Savior appeared to Lorenzo Snow. He then motioned to the water fountain next to us. "This water comes from an artesian well directly under the temple," he said. I took a drink and while walking down the stairs, I thought of the Savior with the Samaritan woman at the well—a person like me with a very complicated background. In that moment, Christ's words seemed fashioned for my heart: "But whosoever drinketh of the water that I shall give him shall never thirst; but the water that I shall give him shall be in him a well of water springing up into everlasting life" (John 4:14).

Sometime later during my mission, I read Ezekiel's vision of the temple and the living water flowing out from underneath it, healing everything in its path. My mind was cast back to that moment in the Salt Lake Temple, and it all made sense. The Savior and His temple were ultimately about healing us and giving us eternal life.

> "We ask Thee to sanctify these [*sealing*] altars, that *those who come unto them may feel the power of the Holy Ghost resting upon them, and realize the sacredness of the covenants they enter into* . . . and that all the blessings pronounced may be realized by all Thy Saints who come to these altars, in the morning of the resurrection of the just."[5]

When I became engaged to be married, there was no question where we wished to be sealed. It had to be the Salt Lake Temple. It had to be "home." I still remember the anxious excitement of that morning. The joy of bringing my bride into the celestial room and sitting there alone for a few moments before our sealing is impressed on my heart forever. Before we headed up to our sealing room, I walked us over to the water fountain and we both drank. I shared my experience there almost three years previous, and we both felt the power of heaven in our decision to be sealed. The words of the sealer further cemented the Savior as the foundation of our marriage. The joy of hearing the sealing ordinance while gazing at my bride across the altar was indescribable. My family was beginning in my true "home." It was the happiest day of my life.

> "When Thy people . . . oppressed and in trouble, surrounded by difficulties or assailed by temptation and *shall turn their faces towards this Thy holy house* and ask Thee for deliverance, for help, for Thy power to be extended in their behalf, we beseech Thee, to *look down from Thy holy habitation in mercy and tender compassion upon them, and listen to their cries*."[6]

On the morning of September 11, 2001, I was sitting in a doctor's waiting room with a view of the entire Salt Lake Valley. Amid that surreal morning, I was watching plane after plane glide from left to right and land at the Salt Lake International Airport. While all civilian flights were being forced to land, reports continued of other hijacked aircraft. My eyes kept switching from the television coverage to the endless parade of planes crossing the valley. From my vantage point, each one seemed headed straight for the Church Office Building on Temple Square with its eerily similar architecture to the Twin Towers. "Is one hijacked?" I wondered. Fear overwhelmed me.

As I returned to work, fear and anxiety continued to build as I listened to the news and worried about the world my young sons would inherit. I drove past the World Trade Center–look-alike Church Office Building, with hundreds of evacuated employees fleeing to safety. As my anxiety deepened, I saw the Salt Lake Temple. In that moment, I felt the words, "Peace I leave with you, my peace I give unto you: not as the world giveth, give I unto you. Let not your heart be troubled, neither let it be afraid" (John 14:27). That intense feeling of "the peace of God, which passeth all understanding" (Philippians 4:7) filled my heart and mind. It was even more surreal than the tragedy unfolding on the news. It was a message of love and comfort from my heavenly home.

> "We thank Thee, O God of Israel, that Thou didst raise up *patriotic men* to lay the foundation of this great American government. Thou didst inspire them to frame a good constitution and laws which *guarantee to all of the inhabitants of the land equal rights and privileges to worship Thee* according to the dictates of their own consciences."[7]

A little over a decade later, I had the two-year opportunity to spend half my working days in the Church's historical department researching for my dissertation. My work focused on the political missionaries of Joseph Smith's 1844 US presidential campaign. Their united purpose was to defend religious liberty for themselves and others. I was searching for as much information as possible on who these men were.

To start each workday visit, I arrived forty-five minutes early to do proxy initiatory ordinances for five names at the Salt Lake Temple. Initially, I did this because it allowed me to park in the Conference Center for free and to be in and feel the power of the temple home I adored. But in time, my desires changed. My research kept pointing to the fact that there were many more undiscovered men who served missions in Joseph Smith's campaign. I realized I needed heavenly help to discover who these missionaries were so they could be acknowledged for their sacrifices and contributions to the Church and for their example of defending religious liberty.

> "O confirm upon us the spirit of Elijah, we pray Thee, that we may thus redeem our dead and also connect ourselves with our fathers who have passed behind the veil, and furthermore seal up our dead to come forth in the first resurrection, *that we who dwell on the earth may be bound to those who dwell in heaven.*"[8]

I decided to start each initiatory session kneeling in my changing locker. I prayed that because I was choosing to do ordinances for those who could not do them for themselves, I would in return have help from those undiscovered missionaries to find them in the historical record. I witness that miracles occurred as I was directed through the mountains of sources in the archives and on the internet. In the end, I found over 300 additional missionaries, almost doubling the total number of known missionaries in the campaign. I understand Joseph Smith's words regarding the work of redeeming the dead in a new way: "For their salvation is necessary and essential to our salvation, as Paul says concerning the fathers—that they without us cannot be made perfect—neither can we without our dead be made perfect" (Doctrine and Covenants 128:15). I look forward to completing this miraculous connection. When the Salt Lake Temple reopens, I plan to do the incomplete ordinances for these men and their families.

> "We praise Thee that our fathers, from last to first, from now, back to the beginning, *can be united with us in indissoluble links, welded by the Holy Priesthood,* and that as one great family united in Thee and cemented by Thy power we shall together stand before Thee, and by the power of the atoning blood of Thy Son be delivered from all evil, be saved and sanctified, exalted and glorified."[9]

After two years of my research, I continued to do initiatory ordinances regularly, now better understanding the often-untapped power that can connect the living and the dead. I performed the ordinances for five names at a time while adding to the temple prayer roll the names of five of my seminary students or family members who needed extra power from heaven. Again, I can testify of the two-way salvific power of performing proxy ordinances. I marveled as struggling students and family members experienced heavenly help and edifying experiences.

"For we without them cannot be made perfect; neither can they without us be made perfect" (Doctrine and Covenants 128:18). I learned that this is not just a salvific truth but a practical one as well. When we do for those in the spirit world what they cannot do for themselves, they in turn can assist and bless us in ways we ourselves cannot. The ministering of angels is *very* real. Those who accept the ordinances are armed with God's Holy Spirit. Seen and unseen, these angels direct us and speak to us through the Holy Ghost (see 2 Nephi 32:3–5).

I have witnessed miracles, greater faith, and softened hearts. I have received heavenly direction to improve my ministering to family, friends, and even strangers as I have faithfully performed the redemptive temple ordinances for the deceased.

> "Our Father, may peace abide in all the homes of Thy Saints; *may holy angels guard them; may they be encompassed by Thine arms of love*; may prosperity shine upon them, and may the tempter and the destroyer be removed far from them."[10]

I witness the fulfillment of the promises of the dedicatory prayer of the Salt Lake Temple in my life. I witness their fulfillment in the lives of hundreds of others on both sides of the veil. Long may the Salt Lake Temple stand as a beacon of the hope and promise of the Savior's redeeming love and work. She is my home.

Notes

1. "Dedicatory Prayer: Salt Lake Temple, 6 April 1893," The Church of Jesus Christ of Latter-day Saints, accessed Oct. 2, 2024, https://www.churchofjesuschrist.org/temples/details/salt-lake-temple/prayer/1893-04-06; emphasis added.
2. "Dedicatory Prayer: Salt Lake Temple"; emphasis added.
3. "Sometimes the missionaries ask this question, 'At what spot in the temple has the Savior come?' And I have said to them, 'My dear young friends, perhaps more than any of you know, the Master has come to many parts of this temple and to all temples. This is the place where He would want to come whenever He visits among His people." Harold B. Lee, *The Teachings of Harold B. Lee*, ed. Clyde J. Williams (The Church of Jesus Christ of Latter-day Saints, 2015), 583.
4. "Dedicatory Prayer: Salt Lake Temple"; emphasis added.
5. "Dedicatory Prayer: Salt Lake Temple"; emphasis added.
6. "Dedicatory Prayer: Salt Lake Temple"; emphasis added.
7. "Dedicatory Prayer: Salt Lake Temple"; emphasis added.
8. "Dedicatory Prayer: Salt Lake Temple"; emphasis added.
9. "Dedicatory Prayer: Salt Lake Temple"; emphasis added.
10. "Dedicatory Prayer: Salt Lake Temple"; emphasis added.

You Have Never Been Alone

Mary Jane Woodger

I HAVE ALWAYS CONSIDERED THE SALT LAKE TEMPLE TO BE THE PREmier temple in my life. There are several reasons for that. The first is that it is the place where my parents, siblings, grandparents, and great-grandparents were sealed, joining the generations eternally.

The second reason for my connection to the Salt Lake Temple is that there are few places on the earth outside of Israel where one can be where Christ stood and walked. The Salt Lake Temple is one of those few specific places on the earth that we know He visited. Because President Snow shared his remarkable experience of seeing the Savior, I can know exactly where Christ appeared, and I have stood in that exact same spot in the Salt Lake Temple.

The third reason for the Salt Lake Temple's significance in my life is a sacred experience I had within its walls. One of the aspects I enjoy about the architecture of the Salt Lake Temple is that there are two sealing rooms adjacent to the celestial room that you can visit after completing an endowment session. Often, after completing a session, I would take the opportunity to sit in those small sealing rooms, either the one up the stairs from the celestial room or the one on the north wall, on each side of the glass doors leading to the Holy of Holies. I do hope that this aspect of the floor plan will remain the same when the remodeling is completed and that those sealing rooms will still be accessible.

One day several years ago, after an endowment session, I was feeling very discouraged about being single. As I sat in the celestial room and contemplated my situation in life, I took the opportunity to sit in one of those small sealing rooms and found that I was by myself. As with other sealing rooms, the "everlasting mirrors" hung on opposite walls. I have been to many sealing ordinances of friends and family members in which the bride and groom were asked to stand in front of those mirrors and look at the infinite reflections looking back at them, suggesting to them that in the mirrors they could see eternity, both what came before and what will come after.

As I looked into the mirrors on that day with only my own reflection peering back, I quietly asked in my thoughts, "Heavenly Father, do you see something wrong with this particular view of the mirrors? There's supposed to be someone by my side. I'm not supposed to be looking at the mirrors all by myself." I then pled with our Father in Heaven, "I am just so tired and weary of being alone. I want to have that person with me and not feel so lonely."

After a few more minutes of contemplation, I walked out of the sealing room into the celestial room and then into the hall. As I entered the hall, I experienced the strangest emotion; I felt lonelier than I had ever felt in my life—a feeling of complete despair and depression. As I walked down the hall, I thought, "This isn't right. I shouldn't be feeling this hopeless in the temple." It was probably the most depressed I have ever felt, and the feeling seemed to intensify with every step I took down the stairs to the hall in front of the creation room. The thought again came to me that I shouldn't be feeling this way in the temple; the temple has always provided me with comfort and peace. Almost simultaneously, I also remember thinking, "I'm so glad I'm in the temple because I wouldn't be able to handle this terrible, sinking sadness if I were anywhere else." It was a sensation I had never felt before—a complete hopelessness and desperate loneliness even though I was surrounded by people. I could hardly bear those few minutes walking to the dressing room and had a hard time putting one foot in front of the other.

As I entered the dressing room, I found myself, once again, alone and looking into a mirror, which was above a shelf on which I could fold my temple clothing. Much to my surprise, as I was removing my clothing and looking in a mirror once again, the Spirit whispered to me, "You have never been alone. What you just experienced is what it is like to not have the companionship of the Holy Ghost. Remember that you have never, ever, truly been alone." At those thoughts, the feeling of desperation and loneliness dispersed and was replaced by peace, hope, and joy as I was once again comforted by the Spirit, knowing He had always been my companion.

Now when I look up at the Salt Lake Temple's beautiful spires and the angel Moroni blowing his trumpet symbolizing the Restoration of the gospel, I am always reminded that it was within those walls that I learned that I am never alone.

Notes

1. On the west central tower of the temple, the Ursa Major constellation, also known as the Big Dipper, points upward to the heavens and North Star. The temple architect, Truman O. Angell, suggested that just as the Big Dipper helps those who are lost to find their way, so too will the temple do the same. "The lost may find themselves by the Priesthood." Truman O. Angell, "The Temple: To the Editor of the Deseret News," *Deseret News*, Aug. 17, 1854, 2.

The Grandaddy of Them All: The Salt Lake Temple

Scott L. Howell

THE SALT LAKE TEMPLE BECAME A CENTERPIECE OF MY LIFE AT A young age when I was living nearby in Draper, Utah. From my youth, I desired to marry someday in this temple, just as my parents had been sealed in the Salt Lake Temple the year before I was born. I remember my mother telling us how much her testimony was strengthened on her wedding day when at first she was told her marriage would be postponed because she couldn't find her temple recommend just as she entered the Salt Lake Temple. She recounts how she broke down in tears upon learning that her marriage would need to be postponed until she either found her recommend or received a new one. It just so happened that at this very moment of desperation and disappointment, the Apostle Elder LeGrand Richards happened to walk by the recommend desk. Upon learning more about the situation, he talked with her privately and then authorized her to enter the temple and be married.

Soon after returning from the Wisconsin Milwaukee Mission in 1981, I joined my parents as tour guides on Temple Square. Each week, I took a shift giving guided tours to visitors from near and far. One of the exciting stops I made was at the flagpole just west of the

Salt Lake Temple where I spoke of the sacred importance of the Salt Lake Temple to tourists. I also did my best to explain the meaning of the stone constellations on the west-facing wall of the temple (so many visitors were curious about why they were there and what they meant)[1] and why only active members of the Church were permitted inside the temple.

A couple of years later, I was called as a temple worker in the Salt Lake Temple and enjoyed serving in the temple for a year or so while attending the nearby university. I remember how much I enjoyed wandering throughout the large temple between my assignments and finding quiet spaces to meditate and pray. I looked at and thought often about the Holy of Holies room whenever meditating in the celestial room. (The lights were always off in the room, and a table with a large vase stood in front of the door at the top of a few steps leading to the room, almost as a sentinel guarding the sacred space.)

A few years later, while I was attending the University of Utah YSA Stake and serving as a ward executive secretary and later as a stake executive secretary, I was invited to attend two solemn assemblies in the Salt Lake Temple for leadership training. I will never forget the electrifying experience of being in this upper room of the temple with other local leaders and the Lord's prophets and apostles. I don't know if I felt heaven closer to earth in any meeting I ever attended as I did in those two solemn assemblies.

I always enjoyed the live reenactment of the endowment every time I attended the Salt Lake Temple. Soon after my wife and I were married, we both attended an endowment session; it was the first time my wife had participated in a live session. She still remembers being in awe of the experience and thinking about how the reenactment is all that the pioneers and early members of the Church had known. For obvious reasons, the endowment in the Salt Lake Temple always felt more personal to me; the actors were real people in a more intimate setting. I also marveled at how much material these older ordinance workers memorized for their role in the endowment, and I wondered if I could ever memorize as much and as well as they did. I also recall feeling great compassion and understanding whenever one of the workers forgot a line and just as much relief and respect for the nearest worker who helped the fellow worker recall the forgotten line.

Speaking of these workers being close, my wife and I will never forget an actor in the session, who represented Satan, sitting down next to us afterward in the cafeteria wearing the same dark suit he had worn during the session. It was unnerving and a little bit too real for the first few minutes, but it remains one of those potent memories these many years later and a stark reminder of the reality of Satan.

My wife and I had a secret dream to get married in the Salt Lake Temple. However, my wife's father was a sealer in the Dallas Texas Temple, and for her dad to perform the ceremony, we would need to marry in the temple in which he was authorized. As we started looking at dates for our marriage, we learned the Dallas Texas Temple would be closed for renovations. Upon learning of this fortuitous conflict, my wife's father announced that there was a chance he could be authorized to seal us in the Salt Lake Temple because his temple was closed but that he would need to send a letter to the First Presidency requesting permission. He couldn't have been more pleased when he received authorization from the First Presidency for a one-time exception to marry my wife and me in the Salt Lake Temple. He also cherished the physical letter signed by the First Presidency permitting him to marry us in the Salt Lake Temple. My wife remembers him saying to her on our wedding day, "I can't believe I get to perform a sealing in the Salt Lake Temple, the granddaddy of them all!" It was in this same temple that three of our children were also sealed to their eternal companions.

While serving as a stake president in the Salt Lake Valley, I arranged for some annual visits to the Salt Lake Temple with our stake leaders and their spouses to participate in an endowment session and then enjoy a meal afterward in the cafeteria. One of the cafeteria volunteers who lived in our stake and whose assignment was preparing and serving meals to General Authorities each week at Church headquarters made arrangements for our stake leaders to meet in a special banquet room in the Salt Lake Temple after the endowment session. These memorable experiences within the walls of the Salt Lake Temple helped unite us as stake leaders and empowered us to better build the kingdom of God within our stake.

I remember well walking the halls of the lower level of the temple and spending time in the hallway where the pictures of previous temple presidents decorated the wall. I always felt a feeling of love and respect toward them, God, and temples as I looked at their portraits. Just around the corner of this hallway was one of the places where names could be added to the temple prayer roll. Many times, I had stopped at this desk in prayerful thought and reflection to add to the prayer roll the names of friends and family who needed the faith and prayers of temple patrons.

Some of my final memories of the Salt Lake Temple, before it closed for construction, include taking my younger children to the baptistry to perform proxy baptisms and confirmations, performing initiatory ordinances during my lunch hour while working downtown for a few years, and attending marriage ceremonies of family and friends. It is this temple, the "granddaddy" of them all, that has had such a defining and refining effect on who I am today. And it was just a couple of months ago, while attending a Christmas concert in the Conference Center just across the street, that I looked upon the Salt Lake Temple—covered with scaffolding and surrounded by tools and machinery—and anticipated with excitement its reopening. I know the Salt Lake Temple situated "in the top of the mountains, and . . . exalted above the hills" (2 Nephi 12:2) will exclaim again, "Holiness to the Lord; the House of the Lord" as it prepares anew a Church and a people for the Second Coming of our Savior and the ushering in of the millennial day.

"It Brings Peace to My Heart"

President Henry B. Eyring[1]

THIS BUILDING ON ITS EAST FACADE HAS THE WORDS "THE HOUSE of the Lord." The first time I walked just a few feet into the temple, I had the feeling that I had been here before. In an instant, the thought came to me that what I recognized was a sense of peace beyond anything I had felt before in this life but that I seemed to recognize and almost remember.

We knew our Heavenly Father and His Beloved Son before we came into this life. We felt peace with Them then, and we long to be with Them again, with our families and those we love.

Dedicated temples are sacred places where the risen Savior may come. In them we can feel the peace of our associations with Him in the life before. In them we can make the covenants which help us to come unto Him in this life and which will permit Him, if we keep our promises to Him, to take us home to the Father, with our families, in the world to come.

Every part of these buildings, and all that goes on inside them, reflect the love of the Savior for us and our love for Him. I felt that one day, high in this temple. I was in one of the towers, in a place few people would have been since the building was dedicated. In a small room that has rarely if ever been used, I saw exquisite pioneer-era woodwork.

I remember the sense of awe that came over me when I imagined the workers who had so carefully carved and finished the detailed moldings. They toiled away without power tools in a place where, for the most part, only the Lord they loved and heavenly beings would look upon it. They did it not for humankind or for recognition but for Him, for His house. They knew, as I do, that He lives and that He asked His people to gather and to be worthy to build Him a house, that He might direct them and bless them and their families.

I know that He lives. I know that Joseph Smith was His prophet and saw in vision not only the shape of the windows for an early temple but the spread of temples across the earth. The Lord has in His loving-kindness entrusted the keys of the priesthood exercised in these temples to His servants, to bless us and our kindred dead and to finish the work for His glorious return. I know that is true, and it brings peace to my heart. In the name of Jesus Christ, amen.

Notes

1. Reprint: Previously published in "Special Witnesses of Christ," *Ensign*, Apr. 2001, 11–12.

PART 4

SALT LAKE TEMPLE WORKERS' EXPERIENCES

Holiness Is the House of the Lord

Kathleen Hinckley Barnes Walker[1]

WHEN I WAS SIXTEEN, I HAD OCCASION TO PARTICIPATE IN A WEDding that was held in a beautiful Protestant church in downtown Salt Lake City. It had all the elements of a storybook event—the preacher in his robes, red carpet down the aisle, rose petals, ring bearer, organ music, and all the rest. I loved it! I felt just like I had stepped into the middle of a romance novel. I was so caught up in the enchantment of it that I began to feel sorry for myself. "I will sacrifice such grandeur," I thought, "because I will be married in the temple. Woe is me!"

It was just a few weeks later that the Los Angeles Temple was dedicated. Because my father had an assignment associated with that event, we made a family trip of it. It was the first time I had ever been in a temple, and I shall never forget the feelings that washed over me when I entered the holy edifice. I stood at the foot of the beautiful sweeping staircase that graces its foyer, and it looked to me like it was coming straight from heaven. All my romantic notions of a wedding returned as I envisioned myself gliding down that staircase, enveloped in love and beauty. But even as I stood there, I knew what I was feeling was more than just romance. It was a feeling of being drawn to heaven, and I was quite overcome with deep gratitude and resolve that someday I would be married in such a place. I think it was then that the temple began to find a place in my heart.

The temple continued to be a special place to me, but it grew even more significant when my husband, Richard, and I were assigned to be temple president and matron of the Salt Lake Temple. This calling led to a number of powerful and touching experiences that helped further my testimony of these sacred places. Almost immediately, we both came to understand that the Lord governs His holy house and there is so much to learn under His tutelage. The great key is to gain understanding of the spiritual meaning of the symbolic teachings of the temple. Consider the Savior's parables—the process of understanding them comes with continuous study, seeking understanding of the Lord's eternal plan for them and their families.

One day we greeted a couple who was sitting in the celestial room waiting for their marriage to be performed. They did not fit the stereotype of most couples, who are young, innocent, and full of the future. The groom was ninety-eight years of age, and the bride was eighty-seven. They had met in the retirement center where they both lived. As we greeted them, the groom said, with tears in his eyes, "Isn't she beautiful! I'm so excited. And I was so afraid someone else would get her before I did. This is just the beginning for us!" They glowed with the love of two mature hearts, taking on a youthful countenance.

This was a beautiful example to me that the temple never loses its special spirit. Whether you are eighteen or ninety-eight, the house of the Lord provides happiness and comfort to all who attend it. The same can be said for a temple marriage; it is never too late to be sealed in the temple. The peace and joy that accompany this special ceremony are not restricted to young couples. In contrast to this older couple who radiated joy, I also interacted with many facing difficult challenges leading up to their temple sealing.

On one particular day, I was a bit distressed to find a sister who looked deeply sad. She was planning on being married a few days later, and her escort was her soon-to-be mother-in-law who spoke no English. I was so concerned about this young woman that I asked a worker to find her after the session and bring her to my office before she left the temple that day. Two hours later she sat in front of me. I began by saying, "Tell me about your mother."

She registered a shocked look and asked, "Why?"

"Well," I said, "she wasn't with you today, and I just wondered."

She then began to weep and told me her family had joined the Church many years ago in Mexico. But since then, her parents and two brothers had made choices in their lives that prevented them from temple worship. She had ended up at BYU and met a wonderful young man from Peru, and they were to be married at the end of the week. And through deep sobs she said, "What should be the happiest day of my life will now be laced with deep sadness because none of my family will be with me."

I was so touched by this young girl's emotion that I asked, "Why didn't you go home to Mexico and be married there where you could be with your family and friends?"

She brightened with resolve and said, "Because I know that my eternal happiness will come from the blessings I receive in the temple, and I am willing to forgo momentary happiness for the eternal blessings that await me."

This was a great lesson to me about the power of the temple. No matter our situation in life, the temple is a place where we can receive comfort, peace, and blessings as we turn to the Lord in His house.

One Saturday evening a young couple attended an endowment session in the temple. The sister who was assisting in that session noticed them. They radiated a deep love and a sense of togetherness. The sister watched them and was so impressed with the "electricity" she felt between them that she determined to find them after the session and share her feelings. She found them in the celestial room with heads bowed. She waited for some time, and when they finally looked up, she approached them. She told them that she had been watching them and was moved by the tender love they seemed to demonstrate toward one another. She then noticed the young man's short hair, and it dawned on her. "Are you military?" she asked.

"Yes, ma'am!" he answered.

And then she said, "Are you perchance deployed?"

"Yes, ma'am. At 8 a.m. Monday morning I ship out to Iraq."

The young wife then spoke up. "When he received his orders, we were devastated and terrified. We talked and fasted and prayed. We clung to each other. In our prayerful searching, we were drawn to the temple, seeking a place of safety and help. It's so wonderful to know that while we are separated, the eternal blessings of the temple will connect us. We feel safe and secure here, and having found peace, we know that we can face the challenges that lie ahead."

The temple is a place we can turn to in trying times. This young couple was such a great example to me of turning to the Lord when we are experiencing feelings of doubt, fear, or despair. He wants to help us, and He will help us if we ask Him. The spirit of the temple comforts and strengthens those in need. However, it is not always easy to rely on the Savior when we need it most.

One afternoon a young woman sought me out and shared this experience. She said that for a time in her life, she attended the temple on a weekly basis, but because all was not well with her, she began to blame the Lord and felt that perhaps she was not worthy or that the Lord was not pleased with her in some way, so she quit going. But life did not get better. In fact, it got worse. In the midst of some deep soul-searching, she determined she would try going back to the temple. The first time back she was apprehensive, not knowing how she would feel. But while she was there, something happened. She couldn't really identify what it was, but she said she just felt better. She began to feel like a person again and had renewed energy. Since that time, her days have improved. As we talked, she suggested that maybe she was beginning to see herself as the Lord sees her instead of letting the world define who she is.

It is such a special feeling to see oneself as the Lord sees you. I have been lucky enough to experience this revelation while in the temple.

There were days in the temple when I would get discouraged. It seemed that the faster I worked, the further behind I got. I could not seem to cover all the bases and meet all the demands that were placed on me. One day, I had the need to leave the temple and return several times. Each time required a change of clothes. I would change from street clothes to temple clothes to street clothes to temple clothes over and over. Late in the day, as I was changing clothes for the *eighth time*, I felt frustrated and overwhelmed. Because of the running back and forth, I was behind in my work. I had not taken care of things I thought needed attention. One last time, I pulled my clothes over my head and turned to look in the mirror. As I did, I had one of those minuscule flashes that come and go instantaneously but speak volumes. I saw myself standing in white in the Lord's house, trying to do my best, and the thought came to me: "It does not matter to the Lord if you do not get through the paperwork today, or do not get to the other business of the day. What does matter is that you are here, in His house, serving Him with all your heart. The little things will take care of themselves." I began to weep, and for just a second, I think I caught a glimpse of myself as the Lord sees me. That was a great moment for me, and when I feel myself drowning in the busyness of the world, I try to remember what is really important and ask myself, "Where is my heart? What really matters?"

In other words, if we will put our lives, our thoughts, our actions, and our hearts in tune with the Lord, and worship the Lord in His holy temple, then step by step, through the gift of the Holy Ghost, the fulness of the Holy Ghost will be distilled upon our souls as the dews from heaven, and we will be empowered to open the many gifts of the Holy Ghost in our lives.

As I conversed with a woman in the temple one day, she shared her experience serving in a leadership position in the temple for the past three years. Yet again, this idea that the temple allows us to see ourselves as God sees us was brought up. As we visited, she told me that when she accepted the call, she was terrified. She had come to this calling with no previous leadership experience. Her husband was not a member of the Church, and although he was supportive, he understood little of what such a calling would require.

And so it was with great trepidation that she accepted the call and went to work. She labored long and hard, feeling inadequate and ill-prepared. But she said that when she finally changed her attitude from "I can't do this" to "I can do this with the Lord's help," she found not only great satisfaction but also success in her labors. She served well, conducting meetings, training other workers, and handling difficult problems. She had soared, and her testimony of the Lord had expanded. And then she made this wonderful and enlightening statement: "Because of this experience I have learned that the Lord can make something out of nothing." Here was a woman who once saw herself as nothing, but when she let the Lord work in her life, she began to see herself as the Lord saw her. It was exciting!

Another lesson I learned while serving in the temple is that the Spirit can be felt in many different places—oftentimes it is felt in the most unexpected of spots. The Lord's house is a place of reverence, and the Spirit resides in reverent spaces. One temple worker expressed her feelings of reverence to me in this way:

> One quiet morning, shortly after I started to work in the temple, the supervisor asked if I'd like to go work in the laundry. As I stepped into that room, I instantly felt such a beautiful spirit. There was clean laundry neatly stacked everywhere, washers and dryers quietly running, and large bins labeled "clean" or "soiled." There were a couple of sisters working on sewing machines, and large folding tables just the right size for standing and folding. The room was bright, and everything was hushed and well-organized.
>
> However, what instantly impressed me the most was the sweet, quiet reverence that met me there. The sisters spoke softly as they greeted me warmly. My first impression was that, even in the laundry, reverence prevails. I love these sisters! The love they have for what they do is eminent. They reverence their calling. They reverence the house of the Lord.

It is through this spirit of reverence that the Lord is able to answer prayers and comfort and prompt those in the temple. One day a patron who greeted me in the temple said, "Oh, it must be so wonderful to spend so much time in the temple. I bet you have had lots of visions."

I thought about that for some time. I had never had a vision, in the context of the way we usually define visions. And I realized that I did not see a vision, nor did I need a vision, because every day I spent in the temple, I had thoughts and feelings confirm to me that the Lord is mindful of each one of us and of our presence in His house.

In the Doctrine and Covenants, the Lord counseled the Prophet Joseph and Oliver Cowdery who were in the process of translating the Book of Mormon. The Lord instructed them in the process of personal revelation, saying, "Yea, behold, I will tell you in your mind and in your heart, by the Holy Ghost, which shall come upon you and which shall dwell in your heart. Now, behold, this is the spirit of revelation" (Doctrine and Covenants 8:2–3).

We can receive personal revelation in the temple if we pay attention to the thoughts that come to us and the feelings we experience in our hearts. So often the Lord uses the things we do and hear in the temple to answer our personal prayers. One brother who came to the temple for the first time expressed his feelings this way: "Before coming to the temple, I was worried and stressed over what it would be like. I asked myself, Would I be able to understand what is taught in the temple, or would I be overwhelmed and confused? After coming, I found that what is taught is so beautiful and clear. I know I have much to learn, and I have a long way to go, but I am excited at the prospect."

Answers come in unexpected ways and at unexpected times if we are prepared. The Savior promised us, "Ask, and it shall be given you; seek, and ye shall find; knock, and it shall be opened unto you" (Matthew 7:7). Our responsibility is to search and ponder and learn as we worship in the temple.

There is inscribed on every temple this statement: *Holiness to the Lord, The House of the Lord.* President Gordon B. Hinckley has said that it might say *Holiness Is the House of the Lord.* That means exactly what it says. When we go to the temple, we enter God's house here on earth. What a remarkable gift to have such a place!

We want to be happy. God wants us to be happy. It is a gift that God offers freely to those who satisfy the preconditions. We want to be with our families eternally and live in the presence of God. Those blessings are promised to those who seek to understand and apply the eternal truths the Lord makes available to each of us in His holy temples.

Notes

1. Reprint: Excerpts taken from M. Richard and Kathleen H. Walker, *House of Learning: Getting More from Your Temple Experience* (Deseret Book, 2010).

John R. Winder: A Blessing in the Temple

Mike Winder

When I was a young history student at the University of Utah, I once enjoyed a delightful conversation with Dr. Hugh W. Nibley, the legendary Brigham Young University professor of nearly fifty years. I told him that I was working on a biography of John Rex Winder for my honors thesis and asked Brother Nibley why his middle name was Winder. After all, there was no genealogical relation between his family and mine. The eighty-nine-year-old scholar lit up and told me a tale that took place in the Salt Lake Temple that no one in my family had ever heard.

The story took place in the early part of 1910—January or February—and the distinguished-looking eighty-eight-year-old President John R. Winder, with his snow-white beard and classy round spectacles, was attending to his many duties in the temple. The prophet at the time, President Joseph F. Smith, was president of the Salt Lake Temple, but because of his extraordinary duties as President of the entire Church as well, President Smith had delegated most of the day-to-day running of the temple to his able First Counselor in the First Presidency—John R. Winder.

While passing through the celestial room, President Winder saw Agnes Sloan Nibley, the twenty-four-year-old daughter-in-law of one of Winder's dear friends, Presiding Bishop Charles W. Nibley. The Winders and Nibleys enjoyed one another's company, had traveled to the Pacific Northwest together, and shared an intense interest in Church finances. (President Winder had been a counselor in the Presiding Bishopric himself before Joseph F. Smith called him to the First Presidency in 1901, having never served as an Apostle.)

While visiting Salt Lake, Agnes was in the sacred temple seeking peace and comfort in what had been a very difficult pregnancy. President Winder sensed her uneasiness and angst and asked if she would like a priesthood blessing at his hands. She welcomed the invitation, and they went into a side room off of the celestial room. "We ought to avail ourselves of the opportunity to obtain blessings there," he once said of the temple in general conference.[1]

In that blessing, President Winder spoke very specifically about the child she was carrying and said that all would be well with her health and the baby's. He declared that she would bear a son and stated in the blessing very explicit promises about the important work that he would accomplish in mortality. The young Agnes Nibley left the temple comforted and eventually took the train home to the Pacific Northwest.

Meanwhile, by late March 1910, President Winder was on his deathbed battling pneumonia at his home (where the Church Family History Library now stands on West Temple across from Temple Square). Some of his final words were inquiring as to whether Sister Nibley had yet given birth to her son. John R. Winder died on Sunday, March 27, 1910.

Nearly 800 miles northwest of Salt Lake City on that very day, in Portland, Oregon, Alexander and Agnes Nibley welcomed their son into the world, naming him Hugh Winder Nibley—the middle name in honor of the family friend and spiritual giant and the special blessing given that day in the Salt Lake Temple. Hugh Nibley would grow to become one of the greatest defenders of the faith and the most prominent Latter-day Saint intellectual of the twentieth century. He achieved distinction as a scholar, author, professor, linguist, researcher, philosopher, and scriptorian.

Professor Nibley told me that "John R. Winder was a very inspired and prophetic man." When I asked about the details of the blessing given to his mother that day in the temple, he exclaimed that they were "sacred," noting, "I have not shared them with anyone, including my siblings." He did note, however, that all of the things President Winder prophesied about him had indeed come to pass.

So who was this John Rex Winder, and why was his greatest love the work that happened within the sacred Salt Lake Temple?

A convert and immigrant from England, John led his family across the ocean and plains to Utah in October 1853. He was deeply impressed when he first visited the Temple Block. "In April of that year the cornerstones of the Salt Lake Temple had been laid," he later recalled. "Little did I dream as I gazed upon those humble though massive beginnings, that I would have charge, forty years later, of the work of completing the sacred edifice, and that I would be an assistant to its presiding authority during the happy years that followed."[2]

Winder became a prominent businessman and faithful confidant of Brigham Young and other Church leaders. As early as 1885, during the dark days of the antipolygamy raids by the federal government, he participated in helping plan for the completion of the Salt Lake Temple. In July of that year, First Presidency member George Q. Cannon wrote in his journal of being bundled and disguised from federal marshals as he took a carriage to the country home of John R. Winder. There, at the original site of Winder Dairy, the brethren met about "the internal arrangement of the temple at Salt Lake City."[3]

In 1887 Presiding Bishop William B. Preston called John to be his Second Counselor, and his role in helping with all Church physical facilities increased. On April 15, 1892—just a week after the laying of the capstone on the Salt Lake Temple and the public pledge by the gathered multitude to complete the interior within one year—President Wilford Woodruff asked Bishop Winder to be in charge of this "herculean task" as General Superintendent of Temple Work.

Future Apostle James E. Talmage recalled of Winder and his new task, "He possessed the energy and activity of youth, combined with the wisdom and discretion that age alone can give. . . . Under his efficient supervision, work on the interior of the Temple progressed at a rate that surprised even the workers."[4]

One day, Superintendent Winder overheard some of the laborers murmuring that there was no way the temple interior could be completed in just one year when it had taken thirty-nine to complete the exterior. He promptly gathered all 250 workers into one room. "I was standing in there talking to them and telling them that if there was a man among them that felt this work could not be accomplished, let him please get his pay and go to work somewhere else," Winder related. "I did not know that President Woodruff was in the house, but it appears that he stood right behind a curtain that was up there, and heard what I said, and throwing aside the curtain he said, 'That's right; the work has got to be done, and if there is anybody here that thinks it can't be done, let him leave.'"[5]

A big part of Bishop Winder's task was helping to raise money to complete the temple. He pled over the pulpit in general conference for donations and personally visited wealthy Saints to put on the squeeze. He also put his money where his mouth was and contributed $1,500 to sponsor a stained-glass window and got four of his business associates to each do the same. (Winder sponsored the twelve-foot-high stained-glass window depicting the First Vision constructed in the Holy of Holies.)[6]

Miraculously, the Salt Lake Temple was indeed completed on schedule and ready for its April 6, 1893 dedication. President Joseph F. Smith said at the event that "no other person could there be more praise and credit attached than to John R. Winder, for his faith and indomitable will in pressing forward this work, and always maintaining that it should be accomplished in the time set."[7] Lorenzo Snow was called to be the first Salt Lake Temple president, and Bishop Winder was set apart as his assistant. When Snow succeeded Wilford Woodruff as President of the Church in 1898, Joseph F. Smith became temple president, with Winder continuing as his assistant.

In 1901 President Smith succeeded President Snow as President of the Church but liked the arrangement at the temple so well that he kept it in place and called Winder as his First Counselor in the First Presidency. It was said that Winder, as the acting temple president in those years, "virtually had full charge of the sacred edifice until the day of his death."[8]

The other counselor in the First Presidency, Anthon H. Lund, saw President Winder at the temple performing countless weddings and assisting with proxy work for the dead for years. "From the day [the temple] opened until the day he left it and was taken sick he never missed but one day, and that was on account of sickness," he said of Winder. "So punctual was he that when they would look at the clock and it would lack about a minute or two of the appointed time, President Winder would take his place on the stand and open the meeting. He was never late, and he was always there; and how the people who attended the labors in the temple loved him and looked upon him as a father!"[9]

In 1902 President Winder drew up the rules that would govern the ordinance work in the Salt Lake Temple for decades. The General Authorities immediately felt inspired to adopt these rules for all temples. They included guidelines for sealings and endowments and even rules such as "People who come to the house of the Lord should be cleanly in their persons."[10]

At general conference in April of that year, President Winder encouraged the Saints to take the names of their loved ones to the temple. "How many of you in this congregation have relatives and friends on the other side waiting for you to do their work for them?" he asked from the pulpit. "Take this matter into consideration and try to make an effort to carry on the work and release those who are waiting for you." Sixteen years before President Joseph F. Smith's vision of the redemption of the dead (canonized as Doctrine and Covenants 138), President Winder taught in that talk about the organization of the missionary work taking place in spirit prison in the hereafter. He declared, "Many of our Prophets and Apostles have gone there. There is an organization there, so that as soon as the ordinances are performed here, the parties are informed of it."[11]

For some time, the First Presidency and the Council of the Twelve had been having their weekly meetings on Wednesdays in the Salt Lake Temple. However, President Winder often had to leave early because "his temple duties were heavier on Wednesdays than on the other two days on which endowments were given." Finally, he meekly asked if the meeting date could be changed to Thursdays. So out of deference to their elder associate, the council voted to change the meeting date. This presiding council has been meeting in the temple on Thursdays ever since.[12]

The General Authorities would throw birthday parties for Winder, the oldest among them, in the temple each year. Each December, temple workers and Church leaders alike would gather in the celestial room for a birthday reception for their venerable leader.[13]

The temple workers were inspired by President Winder's "radiant countenance, his sparkling eyes, his quick step." Winder, in turn, had great respect and appreciation for them and the work they did together. "While the world is ridiculing and scoffing at what we are doing in the temples, I wish to say to you all that every ordinance, every ceremony that is performed therein is of a sacred and holy character," he taught in the April 1903 general conference. "Every ordinance performed there makes better fathers, better mothers, better children, better citizens. Nothing occurs in that house that we need be ashamed of; but everything that takes place there is for the betterment of all who attend."[14]

Oh, how he cherished the Salt Lake Temple—the physical beauty of the edifice, the sweet associations with those he served with, and the sublime significance of the ordinances that took place there. "Brother Winder loved the work that he was engaged in," said President Lund. "He loved the temple work."[15] Quite simply, for its first seventeen years, the Salt Lake Temple was synonymous for the Saints with John Rex Winder. "In the house of the Lord we are nearer heaven than in any other place," President Winder would say, and he meant it.[16]

When Winder died in 1910, the temple workers and his family wore white to his funeral in the Tabernacle as he had requested. His void was so great in the Salt Lake Temple that a life-sized bronze bust of President Winder, cast by Mahonri Young, was commissioned in his memory and sat for many years in the celestial room of the temple. Eventually, the bust ended up in storage, and in 1968 it was generously given to the Winder family by President David O. McKay.

President John R. Winder was indeed a blessing in the Salt Lake Temple. "I was told by mother that President Winder was unlike any of the other Church leaders of his day. He was in a class all by himself," said Hugh Nibley. "He was a singular man, not like everyone else—not by a long shot."[17]

Notes

1. John R. Winder, in Conference Report, Oct. 1902, 82.
2. James R. Clark, ed., *Messages of the First Presidency of The Church of Jesus Christ of Latter-day Saints, Volume IV* (Bookcraft, 1970), 26.
3. David Bitton, *George Q. Cannon: A Biography* (Deseret Book, 1999), 272.
4. James E. Talmage, *The House of the Lord: A Study of Holy Sanctuaries, Ancient and Modern* (Bookcraft, 1962), 149–54.
5. W. W. Riter et al., "Birthday Reception in Honor of President John R. Winder on the Eighty-Second Anniversary of His Birth," 24–25, catalog. ChurchofJesusChrist.org.
6. Michael Kent Winder, *John R. Winder: Member of the First Presidency, Pioneer, Temple Builder, Dairyman* (Horizon, 1999), 184.
7. Riter, "Birthday Reception," 25.
8. Orson F. Whitney, "President John R. Winder (With Portraits)," *Juvenile Instructor* 45, no. 5 (May 1910): 217.
9. "Verbatim Report of Funeral Services in Honor of President John R. Winder: Salt Lake Tabernacle, March 31, 1910," FamilySearch, accessed Oct. 11, 2024, https://libcat.familysearch.org/Record/443194.
10. Stan Larson, ed., *A Ministry of Meetings: The Apostolic Diaries of Rudger Clawson* (Signature Books, 1993), 578.
11. John R. Winder, in Conference Report, Apr. 1902, 90.
12. *Journal History of The Church of Jesus Christ of Latter-Day Saints*, Dec. 22, 1909, Church History Library, Salt Lake City.
13. Winder, *John R. Winder*, 202–5.
14. John R, Winder, in Conference Report, Apr. 1903, 56.
15. "Verbatim Report of Funeral Services."
16. Quoted in Larson, *A Ministry of Meetings*, 364.
17. Author, conversation with Hugh W. Nibley, Apr. 12, 1999.

Salt Lake Temple Reflections

Trevor Wylie

TEMPLES HOLD A SPECIAL PLACE IN THE THEOLOGY OF THE CHURCH of Jesus Christ of Latter-day Saints. The covenants made therein bind families together for eternity and provide a path to return home to our heavenly parents. The work for the living and the dead that is performed within the walls of the temple provides a spiritual sanctuary and a place of peace and holiness for all who enter. The Salt Lake Temple is one of the most recognizable and famous temples of this dispensation. Within this magnificent edifice and on its beautiful grounds, many thousands of Latter-day Saints have had significant and spiritually powerful experiences, beginning with the temple's groundbreaking to its present renovation. I want to add my brief, simple, and sacred testimony to those thousands by sharing a few experiences and thoughts from the time I've spent in and around the Salt Lake Temple.

One of the first experiences that opened my eyes to the importance of the temple was when I visited Temple Square with my grandparents when I was eleven. My grandparents had come to visit us, and my father took them and a few of my siblings to Temple Square for the day. Grandma loved visiting the Family History Library. However, my grandfather was not as keen to spend hours digging through rolls of microfilm, so we dropped him off at the temple and proceeded to go about the day. A few hours later, after visiting the museum, library, and Tabernacle, we met up with my grandfather. I will never forget the simple story he told me of his experience that day. He related that he had decided to perform initiatory ordinances during this trip, and because he knew he had a few hours, he decided to keep going and ended up doing the work for eighty deceased individuals. My young heart was inspired by the faith, commitment, and devotion my grandfather showed me. His testimony of the work of salvation was strong, and he passed that love down to me. The Spirit whispered to me of the gospel's truthfulness in that moment, and I have never forgotten that feeling. My journey toward my own sacred temple experience was well under way because of my grandfather's example.

Fast-forward to 2007. It was the day before I was to enter the Missionary Training Center. My parents and I took a special trip to participate in an endowment session at the Salt Lake Temple. I was preparing to take the gospel to Canada, and I wanted to visit a historic temple with my parents before I began serving. I recognized how important it was to be endowed in the temple and knew I needed the spiritual strength it could provide to fully prepare me for missionary service. And so we spent the early afternoon doing ordinances within the temple. Despite my ever-growing nerves at leaving for two years, that trip to the Salt Lake Temple drove home the importance of why I was going to serve in the first place and helped bring peace to my troubled mind. Satan had been working extra hard the previous few weeks to slow my progress, but this trip to the temple cemented my testimony of missionary work and fortified my decision to serve. I will forever be grateful for that temple trip. I still had fears about my missionary service due to my human weakness, but I knew the work was true, and I knew that it was the right thing to do to serve God as His missionary servant.

Years later, in 2015, I began my master's program and took a job helping the floral department at Church headquarters. Our responsibilities included taking care of the plants within the walls of the Salt Lake Temple. During regular closures, we would go into the temple and clean, trim, move, refresh, and replace plants and trees as needed. The plants at the fountain in the basement, the trees in the ordinance rooms, and the plants lining the halls and sitting areas all needed care. It was always a sacred experience to enter the temple and care for it, even in my small capacity. I knew the work we were doing enhanced the spiritual environment of the temple and created a calming feeling for those who entered the building. One day, while cleaning the trees in the celestial room, I felt an overwhelming love pour over me, which brought me peace and understanding. I knew that the gospel was true and that this was Christ's work on the earth, and I recognized that my small contribution was meaningful to Him. Keeping the temple clean and holy is an important part of the process, and I am grateful I had the chance to be a small part of it.

I started working at the Church History Library in 2018. I attended the temple as much as possible, taking advantage of my proximity to it. As the renovation date for the temple approached, I was excited to watch, almost daily, the progress being made. Obviously, a pandemic shifted how I watched the renovation unfold, but I was still in the office often and could observe the changes to the temple and the surrounding area. In small ways, whether through photos or notes, I have been making observations about how I feel about the work being done and how it is progressing. I feel great excitement as I see progress on the temple. I often feel peace and receive motivation to go about my work in a meaningful way each day. I recognize the hastening of the work and the purpose behind ensuring the Salt Lake Temple lasts into the Millennium. I am grateful for the many hands that are assisting in preserving this magnificent building. I have felt the joy that comes from attending this temple and know that the changes will provide a space for the Spirit to teach and testify of Christ, to those both within and without the walls of the temple. I know this place will bring many closer to their Savior.

I know my Savior lives. In the halls of the Salt Lake Temple, I have felt His presence and His acceptance of it as His house. Though my experiences with this temple are not extensive, each one has been meaningful and poignant. Whether entering the walls and participating in ordinances, viewing the temple from afar, walking the grounds, or working to maintain the place as a holy edifice, I have felt its importance. It stands as an ensign to the nations, a light in the darkness, and a hope for those gone before. It stands as a testimony to me of the work happening in mortality and beyond the veil.

Notes

1. Ezra Taft Benson, *The Teachings of Ezra Taft Benson* (Bookcraft, 1988), 252–53.
2. Doctrine and Covenants 128:4 states, "Then, let there be a general recorder, to whom these other records can be handed, being attended with certificates over their own signatures, certifying that the record they have made is true. Then the general church recorder can enter the record on the general church book, with the certificates and all the attending witnesses, with his own statement that he verily believes the above statement and records to be true, from his knowledge of the general character and appointment of those men by the church. And when this is done on the general church book, the record shall be just as holy, and shall answer the ordinance just the same as if he had seen with his eyes and heard with his ears, and made a record of the same on the general church book."

Working in the Salt Lake Temple

Sam LeFevre

I was called to work at the recommend desk in the Salt Lake Temple in August 2009. A few months later, during a training meeting in November, the temple president asked those of us who served at the recommend desk to consider becoming veil workers as well. Initially, I would serve seven hours (from 4 a.m. until 11 a.m.) at the recommend desk and then three more hours assisting at the veil. Later, I was able to split my assignment into two different days.

During my service as a veil worker, I had about forty-five minutes between each session. Along the south wall of the temple, on the east end, were three small rooms. These rooms were located behind the two sealing rooms that were adjacent to the celestial room and the Holy of Holies that was between them. Veil workers were welcomed to sit in these rooms and read scriptures or visit quietly. One of the sealing rooms and the Holy of Holies had magnificent stained-glass windows depicting scenes of the Restoration (the First Vision and Moroni giving the plates to Joseph) that I liked to ponder.

More often, however, I would go to the sealing office to see if they could use me. They would sometimes ask me to be a witness at off-session sealings that were held in the two sealing rooms adjacent to the celestial room. These were marvelous opportunities to learn about and become familiar with the sealing ordinances and blessings. If the sealing office didn't have a use for me, I would go down to the baptistry to see if they could put me to work for half an hour.

One afternoon, as I was leaving the baptistry and heading back upstairs to get ready to assist with the veil, I ran into the temple recorder. We chatted for a few minutes, and then he told me that my help was needed in the baptistry more than at the veils, and he asked if I would consider joining a baptistry shift. My wife and I joined the Saturday midday shift in September 2014, and we served there until 2018. For a time, we also served as the shift coordinators.

I have often heard temple leaders express their belief that more spiritual experiences and manifestations occur in the temple baptistry than in any other part of the temple. Based on my experiences, I am certain this is true. While serving as the font recorder, I had a profound experience. During this particular time, we had a batch of temple names that were predominantly from Slavic countries. The pronunciation of Slavic names is difficult for English speakers to figure out, particularly if they have never learned a foreign language. In the font was a young man who was struggling to pronounce the names. We had told him that he could just spell out the names, but he wanted to at least try to say them. While we had been instructed not to correct the pronunciation of the names, I wanted very much for the people who would be receiving this ordinance to have their names pronounced as correctly as possible.

As the young man was struggling with sounding out these names, I heard another voice near me say the name clearly, after which I realized that that was the name on the sheet. I felt that as I recorded the ordinance for the person whose name was on my sheet, a recorder on the other side of the veil, but very close to where I was, was also recording that ordinance into the book of life. This voice continued until we had completed all of the Slavic names. This experience very much alleviated my concerns about the pronunciation of names at the baptistry.

During the dedicatory services of the São Paulo Brazil Temple in November 1978, President Ezra Taft Benson taught, "The work we are performing here has a direct relationship to the work in the spirit world. Someday you will know that there are ordinances performed over there, too, in order to make the vicarious work which you do effective. It will all be done under the authority and power of the priesthood of God."[1]

I believe that there are priesthood holders who, when they leave this life, are called to be ordinance workers and recorders on the other side. As ordinance work is performed in our temples, I imagine the spirit of the person for whom that ordinance is being performed sitting on a chair in the spirit world, and priesthood holders, perhaps by the laying on of hands, ratifying the ordinance for that person. The act of a spirit sitting in a chair and receiving the ratifying ordinance constitutes their acceptance of the earthly ordinance.

Prior to 2017, temple worker brethren in the baptistry recorded all of the ordinance work, including recording ordinances at the font and in the confirmation booths and scanning those recorded ordinances into the computer system. One of my responsibilities, at the end of the shift, was to review all of the ordinance sheets to make sure they were complete, scanned, and date-stamped and then to sign a certificate attesting that the work had been done correctly. At the end of my shift, I liked to show the certificate to any youth still in the baptistry and have them look up Doctrine and Covenants 128:4.[2] I hoped this exercise would help them understand the reality of the revelations about the temple that they might study in their classes.

In January 2017 we were notified of a policy and procedure change that allowed sisters, including patron sisters, and brothers of any age to assist with scanning the ordinance slips and patron family name cards into the computer. At the completion of each batch, a pop-up would appear on the screen asking the recorder to certify that the ordinances were correct and accurately recorded and scanned. During our shift, we started letting the youth, particularly the young sisters, record the ordinances. As we coached them through the process and showed them the "certify" button, I liked to invite them, when they got home, to read Doctrine and Covenants 128, particularly verse 14, and to think about how they might be exercising part of the sealing power in the temple as they entered records into the digital "books" and those records were recorded in the heavenly book of life.

I was often amazed at the youth's faithful temple service. It was not uncommon to see the same youth patrons come week after week, sometimes with a parent, sometimes (if they had the means) on their own. We got to know these youths and their families. One young man, who was about thirteen years old when I first met him, would ride his bike from his home in Ogden to catch a commuter train or bus to a temple. He alternated between the Ogden, Bountiful, and Salt Lake temples, and so we would see him about every three weeks. When he came to the baptistry, he wanted to stay for the whole shift. If we were not busy, he would do the work for five names and then get a new set of jumpsuits and repeat. If we were busy, he was so willing to help with temple chores—folding socks and towels, hanging jumpsuits, running ordinance slips from the font to the front desk, or straightening up the scriptures and magazines in our chapel and on our reading shelves.

It was while serving in the baptistry that I started to get a sense of how accommodating the Lord is with His Saints and their individual abilities. Among our regular patrons was a father who was deaf and his hearing daughter. When they would arrive in the baptistry, I would go to the recorder's office to get the ordinance cards for American Sign Language. It was very interesting and instructive to watch how this father performed baptisms and confirmations while signing. Other regulars were the parents of a daughter who was quadriplegic and had some social anxiety. When her father was able to attend with her, he would pack her into the font and hold her in his arms. After the prayer, while holding his daughter, he would go completely under the water to submerge her. If the young woman's father was unable to attend, then her mother would pack her into the font and hold her while a baptizer administered the ordinance, and then the mother and daughter would both go under the water.

The baptistry was always packed on Saturdays. It was not unusual, particularly after the announcement that the Salt Lake Temple would close for renovations, to have a hundred or more patrons in the baptistry waiting for their turn, sometimes for as long as an hour. Obviously, with that many patrons whispering among themselves, it could get a little noisy, but for the most part, the patrons enjoyed their wait studying the scriptures or magazines, praying, or meditating.

A number of paintings hung on the walls of the baptistry, which would rotate every couple of years. One painting by Carl Bloch titled "Christ and the Young Child" was hung just behind the recommend desk in the baptistry. The child in this painting was a spitting image of one of my grandsons, and I would get teary-eyed each time I saw it. A large commissioned painting of the camp of Israel at Mount Sinai hung behind the baptistry reception desk. Sidney King's painting of the Day of Pentecost hung in our waiting area. I liked to invite the patrons to think about how these two paintings were connected. Sometimes they would figure out that the Day of Pentecost occurred on the Jewish Shavuot, which by tradition was the date Moses received the Ten Commandments from the Lord on the Mount. I would invite those who figured this out to contemplate the symbology of temple art—how it teaches us and how connected it is.

We were often amazed at the extent to which parents would go for their child's first temple experience. For example, a newly turned twelve-year-old young woman and her parents flew in from Denver, Colorado, came straight to the temple to serve the Lord, and then went back to the airport as soon as they were done to catch their flight home. I was also impressed when a father, with his new deacon, told me they had gotten up very early in the morning and driven from Kalispell, Montana, passing by a number of closer temples, so that his son could have his first experience in the Salt Lake Temple. I can imagine what a meaningful experience that father and son had as they talked about the temple and the gospel on their long drive to visit us.

While I served in the baptistry, we held a short prayer meeting fifteen minutes before the start of our shift. During these meetings, we made assignments, shared announcements, and occasionally received training from the temple recorder or a member of the temple presidency. Early in our experience, we held this meeting in the baptistry chapel. Later, the number of patrons waiting in the chapel made it impossible to hold our meeting there, so we would sometimes meet in the temple engineers' office, sometimes in the landing of the west center tower, and sometimes in a tiny sealing room next to the baptismal font that very few people even knew existed. These meetings were very spiritual and often brought tears to our eyes as we prepared to serve in the temple.

I am deeply grateful for the time I've been able to spend within the sacred walls of the Salt Lake Temple, and I know that it is truly the house of the Lord.

The Salt Lake Temple: Refuge and Refinement

Milton Richard Walker[1]

AFTER I LOST MY FATHER AT AN EARLY AGE, MY MOTHER BECAME MY anchor, my idol, and my inspiration. As I grew, I watched her work and struggle and toil to care for her four small children. I noticed how she always put us first and often went without so we had what we needed. When we were children, we had a Saturday routine. We would get up, laboriously clean the house, and get ready for Sunday. When our chores were completed, we were eager to get to our play activities. Our mother, on the other hand, would go into the bedroom, pull out a little suitcase, and take it to the ironing board, where she would meticulously press some white clothing. She would then leave the house and go to the temple. We found this so puzzling and hard to understand. We knew she was exhausted from her week of work and her responsibilities at home. We wondered what could possibly have motivated her to go to the temple when she could be home taking a nap or doing something for herself. This became a point of curiosity to me, and I determined that someday I would find out why . . . and I did!

The temple is an oasis in the world. It removes us from the noise, the clamor, the clutter, and the turmoil of the world. It opens a laboratory of spirituality that leads us to inspiration and revelation.

A few years after my wife, Kathleen, and I were married, we were called to be temple president and matron of the Salt Lake Temple. With great feelings of inadequacy, we began our service on November 1, 2005. It was as if we had stepped onto a bullet train moving at high speed. We worked as we had never worked before. We faced challenges we had never faced before. We had demanding hours and consuming responsibilities, as never before. But we also had the most beautiful, inspiring, and edifying experience of our lives. We worked alongside the most dedicated and spiritually committed people who could be found anyplace in the Church. We learned, laughed, and loved. And we felt our lives change on a daily basis.

Our time serving in the temple blessed us with so many special experiences. We came to understand that the temple is all about our Heavenly Father and His Son, Jesus Christ. It is truly the Lord's spiritual university on earth. It teaches us the plan of happiness and opens the gateway to eternal exaltation, which cannot be obtained without the covenants and blessings of the temple. I was reminded of how strong the Spirit is in the Lord's house, and I understood even more why my mother chose to spend the little free time she had in this sacred place. When you spend most of your time in the house of the Lord, your life changes.

One day early in our service, I was walking through the temple to get acquainted with the workers. I went into the laundry and saw an elderly woman sitting at a mangle iron pressing temple clothing. Her shoulders were bent, her fingers were gnarled, her hair was gray, and it was apparent that she was well along in years. As I approached her, I asked her how long she had been performing this service. She looked at me with tears in her eyes and said, "I have been doing this for twenty-six years, and I absolutely love it!"

I stood in awe that day. Here was a woman who for so many years had done this tedious labor, and yet it was obvious that her heart was filled with reverence and love, knowing she was serving in the house of the Lord. Each day she came to the temple was a perfect day for her.

The temple is the key to finding happiness, both in this life and in eternity. It is the Lord's spiritual university on earth, and our understanding of its profound symbolic teachings can be unlocked only through a course of becoming worthy, preparing, searching, pondering, and asking the questions that will open our minds and hearts to the things of God. In the temple, the Lord defines the pathway to the great plan of happiness.

A common misconception about serving in the temple is that it makes one privy to extra perks, such as visions. In the three years that we served in the temple, we never once heard of anyone who had a vision. Nor did we ever see anyone leave with a detailed list of "dos and don'ts" that would answer all problems and cure all ills. The Lord does not usually answer our prayers by giving us visions or by handing us a to-do list. But He does answer our prayers, and He prompts us in many ways.

Sometimes a prompting comes from hearing just a line or even a word in a new way. Sometimes it comes as a calming feeling of peace. Sometimes it comes in the form of ideas that enter our minds and hearts. Sometimes it comes in an expansion of our understanding of the principles taught in the ordinances. At times it may come from observing others. But it can and will come as we prepare our minds and hearts to be in tune with the Spirit that gives revelation and light.

One very important lesson I learned through my service in the temple is that the temple allows us to see ourselves as the Lord sees us, without judgment. We are oftentimes too harsh on ourselves. These negative thoughts do not come from God, and they can prevent us from drawing closer to Him. Heavenly Father loves us completely and without judgment. We need not let our past mistakes define who we are and who we will become. The Lord sees our efforts.

We have often stood near the temple entrance and watched patrons streaming into the temple. Some are dressed in suits and dresses, some in Western attire, some in Polynesian muumuus, and some in the colorful clothing of African nations. People tend to make judgments about others based on the clothes they wear, their hairstyles, or other unusual features. However, when we enter into the house of the Lord, we all clothe ourselves in the same beautiful white clothing, and the artificial judgments of the world disappear. We are seen as the Lord sees us. The worldly accolades fall away. The positions we've held, the letters behind our names, the degrees that have been conferred on us, the plaques that hang on our walls, the titles and accomplishments of the world, and even our physical imperfections fade as we come together as children of our Father in Heaven to learn and worship in His house.

One afternoon, a young woman came to the baptistry to participate in baptisms for the dead. When she was issued the standard baptismal clothing, she asked if she could have something with long sleeves. She had large tattoos that covered her arms and were a source of great embarrassment to her. The sensitive and inspired worker responded, "My dear, the Lord will not be looking at your tattoos today—He will be looking at your heart. Thank you for coming to the temple."

We sometimes find ourselves in the same predicament in life. We have been given all the necessary tools and equipment to communicate with our Heavenly Father, but we let conditions in our lives interfere with our fine-tuning. For this reason, the Lord has given us His holy temple, wherein, if our hearts are pure, we can open the channel of communication through the gifts of the Holy Ghost. Then, as the scriptures teach, we may grow up in the Lord and receive a fulness of the Holy Ghost, and the doctrine of the priesthood shall distill upon our souls as the dews from heaven.

Another valuable lesson I learned while serving in the temple is that we need not feel the spirit of the temple only while we are in that sacred place. We can take the feelings and spirit we experience in the temple and carry them with us through the rest of our day, week, or even year.

A sister from Russia, who had been serving for many years as an ordinance worker in the temple, learned that her mother, who was still living in Russia, was very ill and was not expected to live. This sister felt anxious to return to her homeland and tend to her mother until her death. She said goodbye to her husband and promised to return as soon as her mother passed away, which she expected would be very soon. But when the daughter arrived, the mother rallied and began to improve. She lived for four and a half more years. During this time, a great distance separated that sister from her husband and from the glorious work in the temple. Her heart longed for both. In order to compensate, she talked to her husband every day by phone, and each night when she retired to her bed, she would repeat in her mind the entire temple endowment ceremony.

This sister could not go into the temple for a time, but the temple was in her. Not only did that sustain her in her absence, but when she returned to the temple, she immediately resumed her service with no retraining needed. She taught us a great lesson. It is not enough for us to be inside the temple; we must get the temple inside us.

As I have observed couples and families being sealed together for eternity, I have reflected on my own experience with the power of temple sealing. Because my father died when I was an infant, I have never known any association with him in mortality. I have yearned to know him, and as I grew, I would ask friends and family members what he was like. I had an insatiable desire to know his personality and his personal traits. It was my mother who helped me come to know him. She would often tell me of his goodness and his love of the Lord. She would tell me how very much he loved me and how thankful he was that I had been sent to their home. I have often wondered what it will be like on that day when we finally meet and embrace each other. Because of the great love and teachings of my mother, my heart has truly been turned to my father, and his to me. I have felt his powerful influence for good in my life. My obligation now is to live and serve in such a way that when I am reunited with him, I will feel that I have done all in my power to honor his name and that of my dear mother.

Each of us has become aware that the principle of eternal happiness would not be complete without the results of the sacred sealing powers that bind our families together eternally. Our service in the Salt Lake Temple has embedded in our hearts a deep and abiding love for His holy house. We keenly recognize that for those who will prepare their hearts and lives and commit themselves to search and learn in the temple, there will begin to flow into their lives a river of "living water." The house of the Lord becomes as a "river of life" for each of us. As we drink from its waters, it not only heals us but also links our families together and provides the plan whereby eternal happiness may become a reality.

Think of the implications of that statement. The Lord will plant in the hearts of the children the promises made to the fathers (that is, the promises made in the temple), and the hearts of the children will turn to their fathers. Therein is the great key. Therein is the mission of the Savior fulfilled regarding the "immortality and eternal life of man" (Moses 1:39). Only in the temples of the Lord can the great welding link of families be completed. In other words, if this great work of the temples were not accomplished, then the entire purpose of the Creation of the earth would be nullified.

May we each recognize that our Heavenly Father's plan of eternal happiness finds fulfillment only through the blessings and covenants made available to us in the house of the Lord. It is there, in the temple, that the "living waters" promised by the Savior await us. May we have the wisdom to understand the importance of what is offered to each of us. May we prepare our lives. May we go to the temple. May we search and learn. May the plan of happiness be a reality in our lives.

Notes

1. Reprint: Excerpts taken from M. Richard and Kathleen H. Walker, *House of Learning: Getting More from Your Temple Experience* (Deseret Book, 2010).

At the Recommend Desk

Sam LeFevre

IN THE SUMMER OF 2009, DURING A WARD COUNCIL MEETING, MY bishop read a letter from the Salt Lake Temple presidency soliciting more workers at the Salt Lake Temple. Prior to that time, I had thought temple workers were special holy people (and they are) who were called by Church leaders to serve in the temple. While I strove to live the gospel, I had no vision that I would ever serve as a temple worker. We are often taught that it is inappropriate to aspire to callings, and that is true, but the first lesson I learned from the Salt Lake Temple is that we can aspire to and live toward two callings: The first calling is a missionary—whether a full-time, Church service, or member missionary—and the second is a temple worker when there is a need.

At that time, there were two ways to start the process of becoming a temple worker. The first was to ask the bishop to be referred as a temple worker. The second was to complete a yellow referral card at the temple, which I discovered was available at several locations in the temple. I chose the yellow-card method. (Note that this path is no longer used, and all potential workers are asked to begin the process with their bishop.)

In August 2009, after all the appropriate authorizations were completed, I was called to serve at the recommend desk. The Salt Lake Temple had seven recommend desks in five locations—the main entrance foyer, the temple view room, the baptistry, the tunnel, and the East Gate Building. In addition, the recommend desk workers were responsible for helping patrons in the foyer and waiting area. Because of this, the recommend desk workers were organized as a separate group of temple volunteers and were not ordinance workers. Between ten and twelve brethren were assigned to a typical recommend shift. Eventually, I became a shift coordinator and served in this role until the temple closed in December 2019.

Initially, I was called to serve in a Friday morning shift. Three brethren were asked to come in a few hours early to "open up" the temple. For most of the time I served in this calling, I volunteered for this role. We would arrive at the temple at 3:30 a.m., and the night security would let us in. After changing, we would relieve the night security at the main lobby recommend desk, the baptistry recommend desk, and the tunnel recommend desks. We were asked to complete these tasks as close to 4 a.m. as possible. Security would open the tunnel gates for the baptistry and tunnel recommend desks so that temple workers could start arriving and preparing the temple. They would also unlock the front doors of the temple annex for patrons. Typically, a few temple workers would arrive shortly after 4 a.m., but most would come around 5 a.m. Youth for the baptistry would also start arriving around 5 a.m. Ordinance work started shortly after. The rest of our shift workers would come at 6 a.m., and all desks were opened by 7 a.m.

Often, between the arrival of the temple workers and the patrons, I would have a length of time to really enjoy the quiet spiritual nature of the temple. I would often read the scriptures or the *Ensign*. It was during this time that I learned my second lesson about the Salt Lake Temple. After a time, I noticed that every time I had a new idea, obtained a new understanding, or gained a new insight from a scripture, a conference talk, or an article, the room would seem to get brighter. At first, I thought something was going on with the lights (it is an old temple, after all), but I was assured by the engineers that nothing was wrong with the lights. Then I realized that this was one of the ways that I "hear Him." When I get an insight, and that insight brings me light, I know I have received revelation.

Twice a year, all of those called to serve at the recommend desk were invited to attend a training meeting with the temple presidency on a Sunday morning. We were also assigned to provide a few brethren to staff the recommend desks during the training meetings for other volunteer staff (baptistry staff, organists, etc.) and ordinance workers. During one of these training meetings, the temple president invited us to get a new copy of the Book of Mormon and read it with the temple in mind. My approach was to get a box of colored pencils and mark every passage that related to or reflected a particular room within the progression of the endowment: light blue for the creation room, green for the garden room, brown for the world room, gray (silver) for the terrestrial room, yellow (gold) for the celestial room, red for the sealing rooms, and dark blue for the baptistry. After completing my reading, I was amazed by how many aspects of the temple appeared in the Book of Mormon. I later repeated this experiment, this time looking for the core doctrines of the gospel. The phrase "fulness of the gospel" in the introduction to the Book of Mormon does not refer to a complete description of the gospel. Otherwise, there would be no need for the Doctrine and Covenants or the Pearl of Great Price. Rather, "fulness" refers to richness, and I was amazed at how richly the Book of Mormon teaches the core doctrines.

One of my favorite times to serve at the recommend desk was during conference weekends. It was amazing to watch the literal fulfillment of Isaiah's prophecy (my third lesson): "And it shall come to pass in the last days, that the mountain of the Lord's house shall be established in the top of the mountains, and shall be exalted above the hills; and all nations shall flow unto it" (Isaiah 2:2).

During conference season, people from all over the world came to attend conference, use the services on Temple Square (the FamilySearch Library, Church History Library, etc.), and spend time in the temple. Although at that time, the Salt Lake Temple was an English-only temple because it presented a live-acted endowment, patrons could ask that certain parts of the endowment at the veil be delivered in their native tongue. At that time, the responsibility for ensuring that the veil supervisors knew a patron's language needs fell to the recommend desk worker, and so we would provide the language tags for the patrons as they entered the temple. At the end of a shift, I was always interested to see the number of different languages that had been requested during our shift.

Some of the missionaries assigned to Temple Square would have their preparation day during my shift at the temple, and we would see young sisters from all over the world arrive for the 9 a.m. session. If we saw a sister wearing the flag of her own home country, we enjoyed greeting her in her own language. In my case, I welcomed sisters from Tahiti and the Cook Islands with a *Kia* or *Ana*.

For a period of time, the Provo Missionary Training Center would bus missionaries from foreign countries to the Salt Lake Temple to attend a session before heading out to their fields of labor. For many of those missionaries, this would be the only opportunity they would ever have in this life to experience the Salt Lake Temple.

New temple presidents, mission presidents, Area Authority Seventies, and General Authorities were trained during the week after conference. Some of this training occurred in the Salt Lake Temple's fifth-floor assembly room. During these weeks, I watched the second part of Isaiah's prophecy being fulfilled (and I received my fourth lesson): "And many people shall go and say, Come ye, and let us go up to the mountain of the Lord, to the house of the God of Jacob; and he will teach us of his ways, and we will walk in his paths: for out of Zion shall go forth the law, and the word of the Lord from Jerusalem" (Isaiah 2:3).

The First Presidency and Quorum of Twelve Apostles held their council meetings on the third floor of the temple on Thursday mornings and afterward participated in an endowment session. Several General Authorities were in the temple during my shift. Sometimes they would perform a sealing, and sometimes they came seeking personal spiritual guidance. President Russell M. Nelson was often at the temple to get help completing the ordinance work for names that he or Sister Nelson had prepared. One time, Bishop Gérald Caussé came through the baptistry recommend desk and mentioned that he was there to practice the organ in the third-floor council room. I then learned (my fifth lesson) just how genuine the General Authorities are. These leaders are true leaders, inspired of God, humble, meek, and devoted to His cause. Over the years, I got a few "bro-hugs" from Elder L. Tom Perry on his way into the temple. President Thomas S. Monson loved to greet everyone in his path, sometimes to the concern of his escorts because it could take a lot of time. Once, I escorted President Nelson down the long eastern hallway from the tunnel recommend desk to the lower foyer. He was in his early nineties then, and I learned that he walked much faster than I was used to.

The Salt Lake Temple and Temple Square were destination places. It was not unusual for patrons with valid recommends to come to the temple in a T-shirt and jeans, towing a suitcase behind them. They would apologize for their dress and explain that they were in Salt Lake City to attend a conference that had ended early, they had a few hours before they had to catch their flight home, and they wanted to do something in the temple. We would welcome them in, grateful for their desire to serve. Eventually, I started replying to their apologies with "It's not the clothes that make the Saint—it's the righteous heart. And you are welcome."

Tourists visit Temple Square throughout the year, and it wasn't unusual for some of them to find their way through a temple entrance. Frequently, tourists came to the recommend desk wanting to know if they could take a tour or wander around. We would explain that because of the sacred nature of the temple, tours weren't allowed. But because we had a large front foyer and the temple view room, we would invite them to sit and enjoy the peaceful atmosphere in the temple. Then we would contact the missionaries, and a pair of sister missionaries would come to visit with them.

When my schedule permitted, I enjoyed substituting for other shifts. During one Christmas season, I was substituting at the front desk in the evening. A woman came into the foyer toward the end of the day. It was late enough that the last patrons were already in the temple, so there was very little activity at the desk. She approached me and wanted to show me pictures of the trees on Temple Square that were all lit up with Christmas lights. I think she had taken a picture of every single tree. She was so excited to share her pictures, and I learned that she had had some very positive experiences with members while visiting Salt Lake City. Because there weren't many people coming or going that evening, I had the opportunity to visit with her for a while.

She commented several times that she felt that the temple and Temple Square were holy, special places. She had questions about the temple, and I was able to share my testimony with her about the plan of happiness and temple work.

Perhaps my sixth lesson was that the house of the Lord was not only the Lord's house but also a house for His people. All of His people are welcome to come and learn to the extent that they are able. Some, with valid recommends, are able to enter the temple and learn deeply. Others may only come in the front door but are still able to feel His presence.

I'll share this final experience that served as my seventh lesson. One early Friday morning, right before general conference, I was serving at the front recommend desk. It was the quiet hour, and I was happily reading from the Book of Mormon. I happened to be reading the account of the Savior's visit to the temple in the land of Bountiful. I was interrupted when a counselor in the temple presidency approached the desk. He told me that he had just come from the temple chapel. There, the temple president had weepingly shared with him that the Savior of all the world had been in the temple that morning. He further shared that the Savior loved the Salt Lake Temple. I had learned to love and deeply trust my temple president and his counselors. I am absolutely certain that the great Creator and Redeemer frequently visits the Salt Lake Temple. I am certain that He is guiding the work of His Church—sometimes by inspiration and sometimes in direct interviews. I am certain that He came to His house while I was at the recommend desk. And I am certain He loves the Salt Lake Temple and all that it stands for, all that happens in it, and all those who come to it.

Memories of the Salt Lake Temple

B. Jackson Wixom & Rosemary M. Wixom[1]

THE SALT LAKE TEMPLE IS A SACRED ICON! IT REPRESENTS TO THE world God's presence on earth—a beacon of light for all the world to see. The very structure welcomes reverence as it displays the words "Holiness to the Lord." In some ways, it represents Latter-day Saints through media worldwide.

As we served in the Salt Lake Temple, we felt its international appeal. Even tourists would walk into the entrance out of curiosity to explore this unique edifice. You didn't have to wonder about its purpose. That was written on the faces of temple workers and of the people who were coming and going to the temple. The Spirit was tangible. I remember Elder Richard G. Scott saying that before he moved to Salt Lake City, he would come to the city on business. He would often come to the temple. Sometimes it would be late at night when the temple was closed, yet he would park his car by the sidewalk and enjoy just being near the Lord's house.

On April 5, 2017, we were called by President Henry B. Eyring to serve as the president and matron of the Salt Lake Temple. President Eyring taught us principles that blessed our service. We hung on to every word he said. He graciously explained that President Monson was not well and had asked him if he would extend the call.

At the time, we were caring for Rosemary's mother in our home and were concerned for her welfare. President Eying looked at us and promised, "It will all work out!" During our conversation, he repeated his promise three separate times . . . and miraculously, it did!

With President Eyring's unique love, he expressed the importance of two things: maintaining the purity of the ordinances and helping patrons feel of God's love. He gave us a copy of the temple handbook to study.

Weeks later, when we returned to President Eyring's office to be set apart, he asked us, "What have you learned since we last met?" Of course, we repeated the two main items of instruction he gave us earlier. Then he said, "The most important thing you can do is to live to be worthy of the Holy Ghost. Because if you carry the Holy Ghost, the Spirit will be with you." It was then that he invited us to create a spirit in the temple as if the Savior were around every corner. That invitation guided our service.

We were blessed to begin our service when the new temple training videos were released. They had President Monson's "handprint" all over them! They taught *love*! President Monson said, "It's better to break a rule than to break a heart." This was difficult because temple procedures are so exact. Some temple workers struggled when sister patrons, for example, did not tie their veil just right. It was a time of "loving" over "telling."

Thursday mornings were a gift to the Salt Lake Temple. That is the morning the First Presidency, the Quorum of the Twelve, and the Presidency of the Quorum of the Seventy would meet on the third floor of the temple. A member of the temple presidency and a matron would stand at the top of the ramp by the baptistry check-in to greet and welcome each member of the First Presidency and the General Authorities as they arrived. A member of Church security would stand with us and alert us about who and when each one was coming, either riding by cart or walking down the tunnel. We were genuinely touched by each one's gracious warmth and gratitude—and, we might add, sometimes humor. We felt the power of their priesthood authority. Discipleship is real. We felt their devotion to the temple and the sacredness of the ordinances performed there. Obedience and sacrifice reflect in one's countenance, and it was a gift to witness that truth on Thursday mornings. If there is one way to describe that weekly experience, it would be "abundant love."

We saw miracles in January 2019. The Salt Lake Temple was scheduled to be closed for maintenance for the first three weeks of January. However, unbeknownst to the public, the temple dialogue was to undergo some major changes beginning that first week of January. It would be very easy for a temple with audiovisual presentation to adjust to such a change—it would require just pushing a button. However, the Salt Lake Temple was different. The dialogue in this temple was "live" (presented by the temple workers), and the changes would require the workers to "forget" portions of the current dialogue and memorize new portions. Nothing could be said to the Salt Lake Temple workers prior to that first week of January.

We called a special meeting for all temple workers on Thursday morning, January 3. They had no idea what the meeting was about—except for those who had attended another temple the day before and witnessed the changes. It was announced that we had just three weeks to be prepared with the new dialogue for both the endowment and initiatory ordinances. Since the Salt Lake Temple would be open during maintenance/cleaning, the workers could come in and study the new dialogue privately at their convenience.

We saw miracles! Many temple workers actually made the sacrifice to change their "temple break" travel plans and stayed in Salt Lake to learn the new temple dialogue. We would see workers in almost every corner of the temple reverently learning their parts. "Forgetting" a portion of the dialogue was as difficult as learning the new. Many of these brothers and sisters had been presenting their temple parts for decades.

Enough temple workers were ready to present the ordinances when the temple was scheduled to reopen. It was an emotional day at the Salt Lake Temple. Prompters attended the sessions, ready to assist the presenters for accuracy, but very little assistance was needed. Never have we been prouder of the Salt Lake Temple workers!

On April 7, 2019, President Nelson announced plans to renovate the historic Salt Lake Temple. Renovation would begin in January

2020, and the Salt Lake Temple would be closed and decommissioned after December 28, 2019. This announcement sent a buzz throughout the temple and around the world. With the forecast that the temple would be closed for an anticipated four years, many members felt an urgency to come to the Salt Lake Temple. We experienced a definite increase in attendance during November and December of that year.

As the number of patrons increased, we explored how we could better accommodate them. The large crowds presented a large dilemma. We found ourselves constantly altering our procedures to find the best solution to this "wonderful problem." For example, there were so many women waiting in the dressing rooms to proceed to the ordinances that they were standing in lines with no place to sit. We received a report that some sisters could not stand and were lying on the floor. We found we did not have enough dressing booths and that some women were dressing in the aisles.

We were running low on the rental temple clothing. Clothing could not be laundered fast enough. We were all going into the laundry area and helping fold the items for the packets. Someone said, "Sister Wixom, those sashes have not been pressed!" I had to respond, "I'm sorry—it's more important that they are available than pressed."

The baptistry was another issue. So many youth were coming to the baptistry that we could not get them all in the door. It was decided that we would reduce the number of names each youth could be baptized for so that more youth could participate. However, that meant more baptismal clothing would be used, and the laundry could not keep up with the demand. The temple employees and volunteers in the laundry area were stretched and really deserve commendation for their incredible hard work and organization.

To accommodate the patrons in the order they entered the temple, it was suggested that we give each patron a token as they came in the door. Other temples were using this system, and it worked well. Yet other temples have only one patron entrance, while the Salt Lake Temple had three entrances. This system would not work in this case.

At one point, we considered having the patrons dress and then wait reverently in the large chapel upstairs for the endowment session. However, we realized we would have patrons going up the stairs while new patrons were going down the stairs, creating a logjam. The final solution, which worked well, was to have the patrons, after they were dressed, wait first in the men's instruction room, then move to the endowment waiting room, and then be called up to the creation room. The patrons were very patient with this process.

We did not wait to begin each session on the hour as had been the past custom; as soon as the company was moved out of the creation room, the room was filled again with the new patrons. It was a numbers game! We would carefully count the number of patrons allowed in the company for the creation room, including temple workers. That meant that every seat would not be full because some of the rooms they would move to were smaller.

The Salt Lake Temple workers were incredible! They stepped up to the mark, with some serving two and three shifts a week. They came early and stayed late. At night, we would hold sessions until each patron was accommodated. On a couple of nights, we would hold a 9 p.m. and 10 p.m. session. When we would arrive at the temple at 4 a.m. each morning, patrons would be waiting in the halls. We would begin sessions before 6 a.m. and continue the rest of the day.

Despite all the crowds and chaos, there was reverence—a beautiful spirit in the temple. Many patrons were teary as they walked the halls. Many came because they or their parents had been sealed in the Salt Lake Temple and they wanted to be there one more time. One sister flew in from Hawaii, attended a session, and went directly to the airport to fly home. She just wanted to be in the Salt Lake Temple.

There was no doubt the Salt Lake Temple needed to be renovated. The main elevator operated on a "prayer," and it was a miracle it didn't quit more often than it did.

The very last day of the temple's operation was Saturday, December 28, 2019. It was actually not as busy that day. Perhaps everyone thought it would be too crowded to come. The last endowment session began at 8 p.m. Gathered in the celestial room, none of the patrons wanted to leave. We all tried to absorb every detail of that beautiful room. We prayed that we could remember not only the architecture of the room but also the feelings we felt there. This was a unique pioneer structure, built with incredible sacrifice, and it was now about to be majorly renovated.

Finally, around 11 p.m., we left the celestial room and the patrons quietly began to file out. The maintenance crew, dressed in their white work clothing, were waiting to remove the veil of the temple, which would be the first sacred item to be removed.

As a presidency, we gathered in our office and reminisced about the beauty of it all. Then, at about midnight, the temple recorder, Brother Kent Arrington, came in and reported that all of the sacred ordinance items of the temple had been appropriately removed and that the temple itself had been decommissioned. Now the Salt Lake Temple was but a shell, ready to be handed over to the Jacobsen Construction Company.

Our experience in the Salt Lake Temple was a precious gift and taught us that the temple is a place of personal discovery—not only of the glories of God's kingdom but also of a holy place within us.

Notes

1. B. Jackson and Rosemary M. Wixom served as the president and matron of the Salt Lake Temple from November 2017 to December 2019. They gratefully served with Patrick and Charlotte Price (first counselor and assistant matron), Jon and Bonnie Jeppsen (second counselor and assistant matron), Kent Arrington (recorder), and David Evans (recorder).

"Marrying Ned" Winder: Legendary Sealer

Mike Winder

A FEW MONTHS BEFORE NED WINDER PASSED AWAY, LONNIE GLEAVE, temple recorder of the Salt Lake Temple, confirmed that Ned had performed more live temple sealings than any other sealer in this dispensation. The humorous and legendary Ned Winder was a sealer in the Salt Lake Temple from when he was ordained at age fifty-four on May 10, 1977, until his passing on August 30, 2005, at the age of eighty-three. In those nearly three decades, Ned was by far the most requested sealer in the entire Church, marrying over 4,000 couples in that temple. "His phone was constantly ringing as word of mouth spread of this great brother's humor, spirituality, spirit of ease, and joy," explained *The Skousen Book of Mormon World Records*. "He would be the first to say that who performs the ordinance makes no difference for temple marriages, but it is nonetheless a new Mormon World Record."[1] But who was Ned Winder, and why had he been such a special character in the Salt Lake Temple for decades?

Ned was born a fourth-generation member of the Winder Dairy family in Granger (now West Valley City). His great-grandfather and founder of the dairy, President John R. Winder, had also been a sealer in the Salt Lake Temple during his service in the Presiding Bishopric and First Presidency. Ned grew up in a faithful household, with a deep, lifelong reverence for the Lord's Church and the saving ordinances of the temple. Following a mission to the Southern States and service in the United States Navy in the Pacific during World War II, Ned married Gwendolyn Layton in the Salt Lake Temple. That special ordinance was performed on October 8, 1948, by a family friend, Elder Harold B. Lee, a member of the Quorum of the Twelve Apostles and a future Church President.

"There was a wonderful spirit in the sealing room. It was a small room right off of the celestial room," recalled Gwen. "Both of our moms and dads were there as well as some of our grandparents and aunts and uncles. It was not a large group such as they have nowadays. Elder Lee told us to keep the commandments and to each go at least sixty percent of the way in pleasing each other," she recalled.[2]

The bride and groom enjoyed a lovely wedding breakfast after the ceremony at the Roof Garden atop Hotel Utah (now the Joseph Smith Memorial Building) hosted by Ned's parents, Ed and Alma Winder. Later that evening, a reception was held at the Yale Ward in Salt Lake City, with Ned in a black tuxedo and Gwen in a white satin dress that had been sewn by her neighbor Sister Graff. Governor Herbert Maw and his wife attended, as did numerous General Authorities. The "Winder-Layton nuptial events" were the "social event of the autumn season," crowed the *Deseret News*.[3] But it was that special sealing in the Salt Lake Temple that was most impressive to the young Ned Winder, who always took the covenants he made that day very seriously, even though he famously never took himself too seriously.

Ned worked as a partner in the family business, Winder Dairy. At the age of forty-one, he was called to serve as president of the Florida Mission, and he and Gwen moved with their seven children to the Sunshine State for three years. Upon returning to Salt Lake City, he was hired to serve as secretary to the Church's Missionary Department, where he enjoyed a sweet association with the General Authorities for decades, especially a dear friendship with President Spencer W. Kimball. At the age of fifty-four, Ned was humbled to be asked by his friend, President Kimball, to serve as a sealer in the Salt Lake Temple. The prophet, of course, held those keys of the sealing power and bestowed them upon Ned personally.

The lighthearted dairyman quickly became the most requested officiator in the temple, owing to his humor and spirituality. "He has you inspired one moment and smiling the next" is a common response to those who have witnessed a "Ned Winder Wedding."[4] "I used to think I'd rather be a spiritual giant than a court jester," he once observed of himself, "but that's just the way I am."[5]

Ned would give a unique gift to couples-to-be: a two-dollar bill and a congratulatory note reminding them that they were "two-gether" forever. Another Ned Winder trait was to occasionally turn the lights out in the elevator in the temple as they rode up to the sealing room and instruct the couple to enjoy their "last chance for a big kiss as an engaged couple!" He liked to break the ice with the nervous bride and groom before the sealing in various ways. "I give each couple a breath mint—not because they needed it, I say, but because I know that anyone can develop 'temple breath' that can turn into 'dog breath,'" he said.[6]

"It's a wonderful job and I enjoy it," Ned said. "Usually couples end with a dinky kiss over the alter and I say, 'Oh, I've seen better than that!' After they exchange rings, I'll say, 'Why don't you seal that with a real kiss!'"[7]

The Salt Lake Tribune once interviewed many who were touched by Ned's life, both outside the Salt Lake Temple and within. "We called him 'Marrying Ned,'" said Linda Gillette, whose four daughters and one son requested him specifically to perform their wedding ceremonies. "He was very human, very down to earth. He got their marriages off to a good start," she said.[8]

Ned shared "uncommon wisdom and memorable advice" with newlyweds, said Bruce Olsen, managing director of public affairs for the Church. "Ned Winder was one of those unique characters who had a genuine love for everyone he met and an infectious way of showing how much he cared," Olsen said.[9]

Ned performed over 4,000 live sealings as well as thousands of proxy sealings in the Salt Lake Temple. "Once, I was in the temple performing proxy sealings for the deceased when one of the women in the party passed out and collapsed unconscious to the floor," he remarked. "The couple that was with me panicked; they thought she had suffered a heart attack or something. I calmly told them not to worry—pregnant women faint all the time in the temple. The lady who had passed out was lying as still as if at the mortuary but then sat straight up and said as indignantly as a seventy-year-old could: 'Well, I'm not pregnant!' Then she flopped back down."[10]

The *Deseret News* once published a story about Ned and his famous maroon Porsche 911 Carrera with the license plate "NED" that he drove to fulfill his duties in the Salt Lake Temple every day:

> Winder has been "a Porsche man" for years.
>
> He remembers parking his Porsche in the LDS Church Office Building parking lot and then taking a little extra time to wipe it off. One day, Elder David B. Haight, an LDS apostle, walked by and said, "Boy, you sure keep that car clean." Winder playfully replied, "I wonder if I could have this car sealed to me." Elder Haight's response was, "Go to your room!" Then he chuckled.
>
> Such a reference to the LDS sacred practice of sealing wives to husbands and children to parents for eternity in the temple is a tricky item to joke about. Winder gets away with it, because people know he means it in an affectionate way and that his personal devotion to his church has always been unwavering.[11]

Elder Loren C. Dunn of the Seventy told another humorous story about Ned that took place in the Temple Square parking lot. He saw Ned limping away from his Porsche after parking it the day after President Kimball's historic speech about lengthening your stride. He hurried over to Brother Winder and asked what had happened to him, and Ned quipped, "I stretched a muscle lengthening my stride."[12]

Outside the temple, Ned still identified with his sacred role as a sealer but continued to exhibit the humor that was simply Ned. Son-in-law Bret Bassett shared this anecdote about him: "One stake conference, he was sitting on the stand in his role as stake patriarch. He was well known in the stake as a temple sealer as well," he said. "The floor of the cultural hall had recently been finished with a sealant that days later still had an awful smell. At the beginning of the conference, the stake president said, 'I just want to apologize for the stinky sealer.' Grandpa dramatically sniffed his armpits, to the laughter of the congregation."[13]

Years later, the Jordan River Temple opened, and even though West Valley City was in the new temple district, Ned received special permission from Church leaders to continue serving at his beloved Salt Lake Temple. His younger brother Rich Winder was later called to serve as a sealer in the Jordan River Temple and eventually as a member of the Jordan River Temple presidency. "When we used to tell people about what we did, I would note that the Salt Lake Temple is the only 'true and living' temple upon the earth," quipped Ned. "Rich would respond with something about Jordan River doing more temple work than any other, and we had a friendly rivalry about our respective temples."[14]

"I loved attending his sealings, and I was grateful to be the first grandchild he married," noted his oldest granddaughter, Aimee Winder Newton. "I laughed at his same jokes every time. (Favorite one: Grandma being hard of hearing and when he'd say, 'I'm proud of you,' she would say, 'Well I'm tired of you too')."[15] At Aimee's wedding luncheon after the ceremony, Grandpa Ned loudly instructed her and her new husband, Matt Newton, to 'Eat those carrots. They'll help you see better in the dark!'"

Ned performed the sealings in the Salt Lake Temple for many of his thirty-seven grandchildren, including me. It was a very special day, June 16, 1998, when Grandpa sealed me and my sweetheart, Karyn Hermansen. We wouldn't have wanted anyone else to do the honors that day. In my journal, I wrote, "It was a beautiful ceremony, with a strong spirit present. Before conducting the ordinance, Grandpa gave us some 'last-minute' advice. He focused on three important principles: (1) pray morning and night together, (2) keep a current temple recommend and return to the temple often, and (3) live within your means and always promptly pay a full tithe."[16] He would often share these three principles with couples, sometimes including a silly story about his first argument with his bride, Gwen, when they were debating as newlyweds about whose dad had a bigger lawn to mow, and how they quickly realized things like that don't matter and shouldn't cause unnecessary contention in a marriage. "I remember that Jacob and I were his last grandkids he married, on May 1, 2004," said Jennifer Gurney Wilkes.[17]

A month before Ned's passing, he performed the sealing of my wife's niece Tiffany to her husband, Matt Mulcock. It had been a long day of back-to-back sealings, and Grandpa had caught a catnap on a couch in one of the back rooms of the Salt Lake Temple that sealers could use. Unfortunately, he slept too long and was quite late and embarrassed when he arrived to perform Matt and Tiffany's wedding. After the ceremony, when he joined the family at a wedding luncheon at the Lion House, introductions were made. "I'm the late Ned Winder," he quipped when it was his turn. Grandpa was performing weddings up until a few days before his passing on August 30, 2005.

Ned had been involved in so many civic, business, and Church assignments throughout his life that when word reached the First Presidency that he had died, President Gordon B. Hinckley quipped, "Well, that's the only thing he hasn't done yet!" President James E. Faust added at the funeral, "I don't know anyone who had quite the zest for living life and loving others like Ned Winder."[18] In a letter to Ned's widow, Gwen, Presidents Hinckley, Monson, and Faust declared, "We appreciate his faithfulness, which was demonstrated in Church service in various capacities throughout his life including full-time missionary, twenty-one years as secretary with the Church's Missionary Department, mission president three times, stake patriarch, and sealer in the Salt Lake Temple."[19] Even to the First Presidency, Ned's service in the temple was the crown of a most distinguished career.

Ned's fellow ward members in the Jordan North Second Ward also mourned his loss, as so many of them had experienced a "Ned Winder Wedding" for themselves, friends, or family members. "Ned will be remembered as a joyful, fun-loving, generous giant in our community," eulogized the ward newsletter. "Hundreds of couples know him as the sealer who made their families eternal. He was known as 'Marryin' Sam' by the Salt Lake Temple workers and was considered the busiest sealer in the whole church."[20]

Notes

1. Paul B. Skousen, *The Skousen Book of More Amazing Mormon World Records* (Cedar Fort, 2008), 103; also an email exchange between the author and Paul Skousen, Feb. 4, 2005.
2. Quoted in Mike Winder, *A Celebration of a Life: Gwendolyn Leone Layton Winder* (n.p., 2016), 43.
3. "Gwen Layton, Ned Winder Wed," *Deseret News*, Oct. 9, 1948.
4. Bret R. Bassett and Michael K. Winder, *Ned Winder: The Antics and Adventures of a Utah Legend* (n.p., 2002), 92.

5. Dennis Lythgoe, "Stories Show Raconteur Loves a Walk on Light Side," *Deseret News*, Nov. 17, 1995.
6. Bassett and Winder, *Ned Winder*, 93.
7. Bassett and Winder, *Ned Winder*, 93–94.
8. Cathy McKitrick, "A Utahn Who 'Truly Loved People,'" *Salt Lake Tribune*, Aug. 31, 2005, C1.
9. McKitrick, "Truly Loved People," C1.
10. Bassett and Winder, *Ned Winder*, 94.
11. Lythgoe, "Walk on Light Side."
12. Bassett and Winder, *Ned Winder*, 87.
13. "Memories of Ned Shared by His Family on His 92nd Birthday," FamilySearch (Edwin Cannon Winder), accessed Oct. 11, 2024, https://www.familysearch.org/photos/artifacts/8442421.
14. Bassett and Winder, *Ned Winder*, 103–4.
15. "Memories of Ned."
16. *The Journal of Michael K. Winder: Volume I as a Married Man*, 9, in author's possession.
17. "Memories of Ned."
18. Quoted by President James E. Faust in remarks at Ned Winder's funeral, Sept. 2, 2005, audio file online at "14 Special Speaker-President Faust.mp3," FamilySearch (Edwin Cannon Winder), accessed Oct. 11, 2024, https://www.familysearch.org/tree/person/memories/KWCP-68Z.
19. Letter from the First Presidency to Gwen Winder, Aug. 31, 2005, copy online at "First Presidency Letter to Gwen at Ned's Passing - Aug. 31, 2005," FamilySearch (Edwin Cannon Winder), accessed Oct. 11, 2024, https://www.familysearch.org/tree/person/memories/KWCP-68Z.
20. "Jordan North 2nd Ward Newsletter at Ned's Passing - Sept. 2005," FamilySearch (Edwin Cannon Winder), accessed Oct. 11, 2024, https://www.familysearch.org/tree/person/memories/KWCP-68Z.

Part 5

Looking Forward

Touching the Temple

Mark D. Ogletree

"As we touch the temple, the temple will touch us."
—President Thomas S. Monson

MANY YEARS AGO, AS A RELIGIOUS EDUCATOR, I CAME ACROSS A STORY that has truly transformed my life and, subsequently, the lives of many others. While serving as a counselor in the First Presidency in 1957, President Harold B. Lee shared the following experience. He explained that a watchman on Temple Square in Salt Lake City gave him a note that contained the following experience:

> One morning not so long ago I was sitting at the desk of the temple gate house reading when my attention was drawn to a knock on the door. There stood two little boys, aged about seven or eight years. As I opened the door, I noticed that they were poorly dressed and had been neither washed nor combed. They appeared as if they had left home before father or mother had awakened that morning. As I looked beyond these little fellows, I saw two infants in pushcarts. In answer to my question as to what they wanted, one of the boys pointed to his little brother in the cart and replied: "His name is Joe. Will you shake hands with little Joe? It is little Joe's birthday—he is two years old today, and I want him to touch the temple so

when he gets to be an old man he will remember he touched the temple when he was two years old."

Pointing to the other little boy in the other cart, he said this: "This is Mark, he's two years old, too." Then, with a solemn, reverent attitude rare in children so young, he asked, "Now can we go over and touch the temple?" I replied: "Sure you can." They pushed their little carts over to the temple and lifted the infants up, and placed their hands against that holy building. Then as I stood there with a lump in my throat, I heard the little boy say to his infant brother, "Now, Joe, you will always remember when you was two years old you touched the temple." They thanked me and departed for home.[1]

It is moving to consider two boys, seven or eight years of age, waking up early in the morning to make their way to the Salt Lake Temple. The parents of these young boys were most likely still asleep. Perhaps they did not even know their sons were missing. I try to imagine these young boys pulling two young toddlers, Joe and Mark, some distance in pushcarts or strollers all the way to the Salt Lake Temple. Their mission was a simple one. All they hoped to do was provide an opportunity for their young brothers to touch the house of the Lord. One cannot hear of this experience without feeling a sense of sacredness and respect.

Not long after reading this story and sharing it with my students, I began to consider what this experience could mean for our family. My wife, Janie, and I considered how touching the temple could bless our children. After all, they were too young to go inside the temple, but we felt that touching the temple at their young age could have a significant impact on their lives. We lived in Mesa, Arizona, at the time and often brought our children to the temple grounds to feel the Spirit and to spend time in the visitor's center. Now, we enjoyed the added blessing of touching the temple. During this time, we would often travel between Mesa, Arizona, and Provo, Utah. On those frequent drives, we would stop at the Manti Temple grounds and allow our children to run around, stretch their legs, and touch the temple.

As our children became older and we traveled more, we would try to locate the temple in whatever area we were in. We would find the temple, stop the car, and have our children touch the sacred building.

I'm not sure what the long-term impact will be on our children and grandchildren as they continue to touch the temples; however, at least our children know one thing—that the temple was important enough to their parents that they were willing to adjust their travel plans to make sure that their children set foot on those temple grounds and touched the temple.

Over the years, our children have touched many temples, including the following:

- Salt Lake City
- Provo
- Manti
- Logan
- Idaho Falls
- Mt. Timpanogos
- Mesa
- Los Angeles
- Houston
- Dallas
- San Antonio
- Washington D.C.
- Monticello
- Nauvoo
- Kansas City
- Denver
- St. George
- Orlando
- San Diego
- Newport Beach
- Seattle
- Rexburg
- Rome
- Saratoga Springs

As our children became older and began having children of their own, we included our grandchildren in the tradition. Our family will continue to find and visit temples throughout the world. We will follow the legacy left by the brothers of "Little Joe" and "Mark" as our children carry on the same tradition. And even though our children are grown and gone, Janie and I continue to find temples when we travel. And if we cannot attend a session, at least we can touch the temple. Just recently, I was invited to speak at a conference in Australia. My wife, Janie, and I made sure that we stopped at the Melbourne Australia Temple to touch it and to share the photo with our grandchildren.

In 2020 I was called to be the president of the Edgemont North Stake in Provo, Utah. I wanted to pass down the tradition of touching the temple to our stake members. In a recent stake conference, we declared 2023 to be the year of the temple. During one session, I shared the story of Little Joe and Mark touching the Salt Lake Temple. In addition to encouraging our members to attend the temple more than they had in the past, we also encouraged them to "touch" the temple with their families and to share their photos with our stake presidency. The result was incredible. Over a hundred families sent us photographs of their families touching temples across the country, from California to New York. We also received photos of many members touching temples on almost every continent, from Asia to Europe.

In a general conference message years ago, President Thomas S. Monson related the story of a grandfather who took his granddaughter, on her birthday, not to the zoo or to the movies but to the temple grounds: "The two walked to the large doors of the temple. He suggested that she place her hand on the sturdy wall and then on the massive door. He said to her, 'Remember that this day you touched the temple. One day you will go inside.' His gift to the little one was not candy or ice cream but an experience far more significant and everlasting—an appreciation of the house of the Lord. She had touched the temple, and the temple had touched her."[2]

It sounds like this grandfather may have read the story of Little Joe and Mark. As our children and grandchildren touch the temple, the temple will touch us, move us, inspire us, and become a significant part of our lives.

Notes

1. Harold B. Lee, "A Birthday to Remember," *Ensign*, Feb. 2971, 35. See also Harold B. Lee, in Conference Report, Apr. 1957, 21.
2. Rosemary Wixom, "Three Ways You Can Prepare Your Children for the Temple," *Church News*, Feb. 3, 2014.

A Proud Monument of the Saints' Faith, Perseverance, and Industry

Maclane Heward & James Smith

Brigham Young declared of the Salt Lake Temple, "I want to see that temple built in a manner that it will endure through the millennium. And when the millennium is over . . . I want that temple still to stand as a proud monument of the faith, perseverance, and industry of the saints of God in the mountains, in the nineteenth century."[1]

What a beautiful vision! To facilitate the accomplishment of this vision, the Church closed the Salt Lake Temple in December 2019 to begin a massive project to strengthen its structure. This chapter will consist of four sections explaining the following topics: (1) the early Saints' commitment to building a lasting temple, (2) why the Church may have decided to undertake this project at this time, (3) what the project entails, and finally, (4) what spiritual principles and truths this project can illuminate.

Commitment of the Early Saints

Brigham Young was not alone in his desire to build a long-lasting House of God. During the October 1852 general conference, a public discussion was held about the building materials to be used for the temple. Heber C. Kimball suggested a few different materials for the Saints to consider: sandstone, which had been used to build the block wall surrounding Temple Square; adobe, which had been used in the construction of the tithing office; and oolite, a sedimentary rock formed of very small spherical grains of which a deposit had been recently found in Sanpete County. All of these were possible building materials. After some discussion, Heber C. Kimball stood and declared a motion to "build a Temple of the best materials that can be obtained in the mountains of North America, and that the [First] Presidency dictate where the Stone and other materials shall be obtained."[2] The motion was supported by members of the Church. However, the question remained: would they be willing to put forth the necessary effort and sacrifice to complete a building with such high expectations?[3]

Brigham Young, seemingly nervous about the significance of the sacrifice, responded by indicating that if the Saints wanted a temple of the strongest material, they would need to build it from "platina" [platinum], something he thought was not found in the territory. If not platinum, then gold. If the Saints wanted to build the temple with the *best* material, "they [would] have to put into the tithing stores something besides old half-dead stinking cows, and old broken-kneed horses; or if they even put in all the good cattle they possess, will it build a temple of gold, of silver, or of brass? No, it will not."[4] Then, acknowledging the commitment of the Saints to build the temple of the best material, he said, "As for the temple, I will give you the nature of your vote with regard to it. . . . But I give it as my opinion that adobies [adobe] are the best article to build it of." While expressing his opinion, Brigham also declared that he did "not fear the expense, neither do I care what you build it of; only when it is built, I want it to stand, and not fall down and decay in twenty or thirty years." Brigham then quoted John Taylor, agreeing that when he died and arrived "within the veil into the heavenly world," he wants to "not be ashamed of it."[5] And so it was agreed that the temple would be built of the best materials and the best practices available to the Saints at the time. This initial commitment made certain decisions easier, such as reconstructing certain portions of the temple foundation after finding it had settled during its burial at the time of the Utah War. It may have also slowed the construction process because the Saints were unwilling to cut corners in quality to hasten completion. In the end, the temple was built of the best materials and processes available to them at the time and has remained a powerful testament to the "faith, perseverance and industry of the Saints of God" for more than 130 years.

Why Now?

From time to time the First Presidency will ask the Presiding Bishopric to evaluate and report on the state and stability of the Salt Lake Temple. When Elder Gary E. Stevenson was serving in the Presiding Bishopric in 2015, the temple was evaluated and given a review by the Bishopric that reads, in part, "In the design and construction of the Salt Lake Temple, the best engineering, skilled labor, construction materials, furnishings, and other period-available resources were used." It was, in effect, just as the early Saints had desired. The temple architect, Truman Angell, had used up-to-date architectural textbooks and even traveled to Europe to study cathedrals and other buildings that had lasted the test of time.[6] The report explained that "the granite exterior and interior floor joists and support beams are in good condition" and that "recent studies confirm that the location chosen by Brigham Young for the temple has very good soils and excellent compaction qualities."[7] Despite these realities, the report recommended updating obsolete utility systems and exterior decking, among other things. The Presiding Bishopric also recommended that the First Presidency consider a "more comprehensive seismic upgrade beginning from the temple foundation on upward."[8]

"To some extent, buildings are like people," explained President Nelson when the temple renovation was announced in 2019. "Not only is the aging process inevitable, but it can also be unkind. The good news is that buildings can be renovated. The bad news is that needed renovations take time."[9] In 2021 President Nelson further discussed the stability of the temple and its need for renovation. He noted that "these many decades later, however, if we examine the foundation closely, we can see the effects of erosion, gaps in the original stonework, and varying stages of stability in the masonry."[10] The original foundation was put into place by relatively unskilled laborers who were not necessarily experts in masonry. The difficulties of their undertaking were expanded by material shortages; insufficient mortar, for example, may have been a significant factor in the original settling of the temple, identified in 1859 when it was uncovered after the Utah War.[11] The resulting effects of time, available resources, and unskilled labor resulted in, as President Nelson detailed, erosion, settling, and gaps in the stone foundation, which necessitated the renovation.

Similarly, President Nelson noted that the temple was vulnerable to the forces of nature. As highlighted in the Presiding Bishopric's 2015 report, these forces specifically include earthquakes and their potentially devastating effects. President Nelson's statements during the initial announcement indicated the Church's commitment to see that the temple, as much as possible, could withstand seismic stress. This was illustrated in dramatic effect on March 18, 2020, just three months after the beginning of the renovations, when a 5.7-magnitude earthquake hit Magna, Utah, just fifteen miles away from the temple. The most visible damage caused to the temple during the earthquake was to the statue of angel Moroni, whose trumpet was shaken from his grasp, falling onto a ledge not far from his position.[12] While no one was hurt, there was minor displacement of a few small stones on the temple spires. Daniel Woodruff, a Church spokesman, said that the earthquake "emphasizes why this project is so necessary to preserve this historic building and create a safer environment for all visitors."[13]

Strengthening the Temple

Strengthening the Salt Lake Temple was a complicated, multi-stage process. In the case of an earthquake, the temple would experience two types of challenges. First, if the foundation fails, then the building itself would become unstable and unsafe or, worse, it may completely collapse. Second, if the foundation stays intact, the structure may still experience cracks and destabilization as parts of the building move independently of each other. The overall objective of the renovations was to overcome these two potentially devastating byproducts of seismic activity by, first, tying the temple together as one unified structure (i.e., structural reinforcement), and second, to place the temple on a new foundation that will allow it to move, or perhaps remain in place, independent of the earth beneath it (i.e., base isolation). In the end, the temple has the capacity to move horizontally up to five feet in the opposite direction of the earth below.

This dual-purpose strengthening process can be described in a series of twelve steps[14]:

1. *Expose the original foundation.* This excavation process allowed contractors to better understand the state of the original foundation, which revealed the specific needs of strengthening the foundation and filling several gaps between the original stonework caused by erosion and settling.

2. *Strengthen the original foundation.* First, holes were drilled at different angles into the original rough-cut stones. Then, these holes were filled with high-strength grout (a type of concrete) to permeate the entire foundation and fill gaps and voids as needed. In some cases, steel rods were inserted and post-tensioned to improve strength and unify the original foundation. The post-tensioning process, an increasingly common approach in modern concrete work, allows the contractor to essentially squeeze the massive stones together from the outside to ensure solidarity and connectiveness of the foundation. This is akin to trying to move a large stack of books from one shelf to another. If you can press your hands tightly enough on the top and bottom of the stack of books, the applied force can keep the books together. The cables running through the concrete, when pulled at the right moment, add the needed tension to the concrete, dramatically improving its strength.

3. *Shoring for continuing excavation.* Because the ground directly underneath and to the sides of the temple needed to be removed as part of the renovation, a shoring wall consisting of interlocking concrete piers that are reinforced with steel columns was put in place around the outside of the foundation. This wall keeps the soil that is under the original temple foundation from collapsing under the extreme weight of the temple (estimated to be 187 million pounds) while the surrounding excavation work continued.

4. *"Jack and bore."* Once excavation around the temple was completed, large cylindrical pipes were painstakingly inserted horizontally underneath the temple. Inside the tight quarters of these large steel pipes, workers dug tunnels in front of the large pipes with

small shovels and picks, inch by inch, underneath the temple to create space for these pipes to be pushed into place. This process is nicknamed "jack and bore."[15] *Jack* refers to the pipes being slowly jacked into place, and *bore* refers to the tunnel boring process being completed by the workers within the pipes. Once the boring process was completed and the pipe was in place underneath the temple, high-strength concrete, steel reinforcing, and piping for additional post-tensioning cables were then installed into the newly created cavities. Ultimately, the temple rests on these cylindrical beams, and in the coming steps, the weight of the temple will be transferred to the new, still-to-come lower foundation.

5. *Additional shoring walls.* Once the cylindrical beams were in place, another shoring wall was then added to the inside of the temple so that the dirt on both the inside and the outside could be excavated to a new depth of seventeen feet below the original foundation. This is the depth of the new foundation upon which the base isolators will be located.[16]

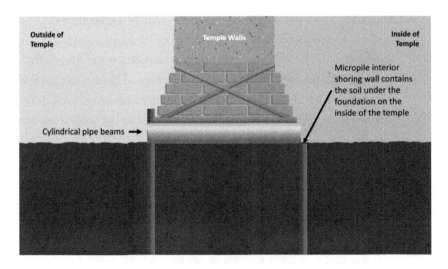

6. *Form and pour a new lower foundation.* The new, lower foundation was then constructed on the inside and outside of the shoring walls, keeping in place the dirt directly underneath the temple. This new foundation consists of six-foot-thick concrete footings with reinforcing steel bars. As mentioned in step 5, the ninety-eight base isolators are then installed on this foundation. Each base isolator

is seven feet across and weighs 18,000 pounds and can hold more than eight million pounds.

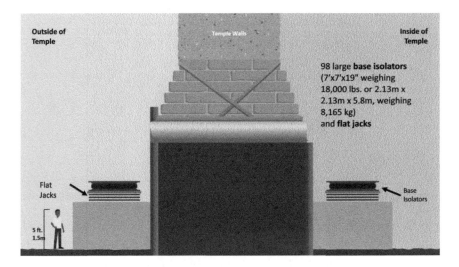

7. *Install concrete transfer beams.* Concrete transfer beams were then installed on top of the base isolators. These transfer beams are similarly reinforced by enormous amounts of steel and post-tensioned cables and then connected to the underpinning cylindrical beams installed beneath the original foundation, as detailed in step 4.

8. *Add post-tension steel cables.* Steel cables were inserted into the pre-installed ducts that run through the large cylindrical pipes from step 4. These cables were tensioned, or pulled, to dramatically increase the strength of the concrete and create an upward force. This process tied together the original temple foundation (step 2), the cylindrical beams (step 4), and the transfer beams (step 7), allowing the weight of the temple to be transferred onto the new base isolators and foundation.

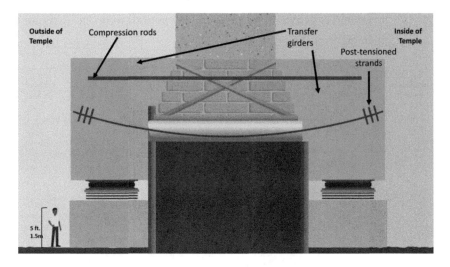

9. *Remove shoring walls.* As the weight of the temple was transferred to the base isolators, the dirt and the shoring walls underneath the upgraded initial foundation needed to be removed so that the temple would have the capacity to move independently of the earth below it.

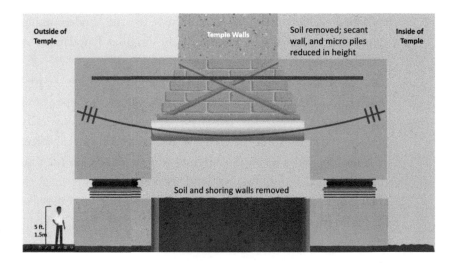

10. *Install roof-level bonding beams and steel roof trusses.* Since the building above the foundation consists of large granite blocks, primarily using the force of gravity to stay in place, the rest of the building would potentially still crumble in the case of an earthquake. To remedy this, large concrete bonding beams were

built on both outside walls at the roof level, and new steel roof trusses were installed on both sides of the original trusses. These additional trusses bear on the bonding beams, support the weight of the new mechanical systems, and bind the walls and towers together at the roof level.

11. *Unify walls.* With the roof system now connected with the towers and the foundation secured, it was now the walls' turn to be integrated in order to complete the unification. To do this, long holes were drilled with incredible accuracy through the exterior walls of the temple all the way into the newly strengthened foundation. These holes run from the top of the temple to the new foundation. Post-tensioned steel cables were installed in these holes to connect the walls with the foundation as well as the roof structure. These cables serve to bind the walls together with the new foundation and roof structure.

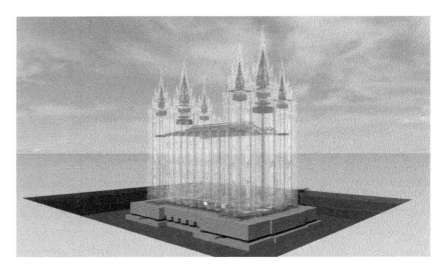

12. *Add structural reinforcement to the towers.* The final step was to add structural steel reinforcement up to the very top of each of the towers, ensuring that the entire building operates as a single unit in the case of an earthquake. The original exterior stone facade of the towers was removed from the original structure and reinstalled on custom-built steel tower components. The newly fabricated steel spires will be clad in the original stonework, including the original capstone, all of which were carefully mapped, removed, cataloged,

cleaned, and stored in anticipation of their returning to the top of the temple near the end of the renovation process.[17]

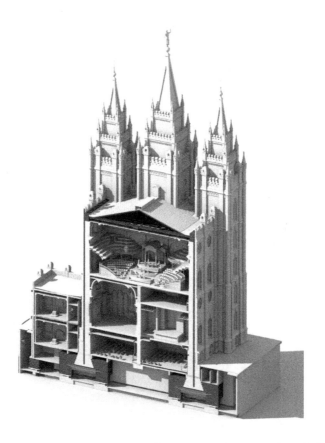

These steps give an overview of a very sophisticated and delicate project that required incredible skill, immense planning, and years of hard work. Workers from around the world, on both the original construction and the renovation, should be hailed for their sacrifice, detail, and careful, expert efforts.

Spiritual Parallels

Perhaps not surprisingly, since "all things bear record of [God]" (Moses 6:63; Alma 30:44), the Salt Lake Temple's physical renovation is not without its own unique spiritual parallels. As mentioned above, the extraordinary engineering and construction efforts of many aimed to accomplish two primary objectives: (1) to unify the existing structure from the highest point to the lowest point, and (2) to quite literally isolate, or disconnect, the structure itself from the earth below it. Both of these objectives contain beautiful and instructive spiritual insights.

Unify the Structure

The unification process of the Salt Lake Temple echoes the Apostle Paul's teachings about the critical need for the body of Christ to be one, despite the necessity of different members (1 Corinthians 12:14–31). Each part of the building, from foundations to exterior facades to carpentry to paint, needs the other to be considered complete according to the designer's intent. Each aspect plays a critical, albeit different, role in achieving the ultimate purpose of the building and allowing it to perform its intended function. Each of these components are carefully and meticulously planned and coordinated during the course of the construction process.

Similarly, the Creator of heaven and earth planned and coordinated the lives of his children, each bestowed with differing gifts and talents. Each of us, as different pieces of His plan, play a part in accomplishing the Designer's ultimate intent, His work and His glory—the immortality and eternal life of man (Moses 1:39). The process of becoming perfect necessitates our differences. But like the body of Christ analogy, the Savior also admonishes us to "be one, even as [the Father and I] are one" (John 17:22). The temple's renovation exemplifies the importance of being one, a single structure made up of many different parts, that we may weather the movements and storms of the world around us and remain unified as the body of Christ. Paul also captured this idea when he taught, "Now are they many members, yet but one body" (1 Corinthians 12:20).

Disconnect from the Earth

In most foundation analogies used in gospel teaching, including those given as recently as April 2024 (by Elder David A. Bednar) and as anciently as Christ's teaching of the foolish man versus the wise man (Matthew 7:24–29), the idea is to attach the foundation of our structure securely to the rock (Helaman 5:12). In this typical analogy, the rock represents Jesus Christ. The Savior, as the source of truth and light, creates the perfect, immovable base to which we strive to anchor our souls. Unfortunately, unlike these inspirational and instructive analogies, the risky reality for the Salt Lake Temple is that the rock foundation upon which it is built might actually move! This reality gives us a chance to consider a slightly altered version of the well-taught foundation analogy—the idea of stillness, found in Christ, in the midst of a potentially volatile and erratic world.

The temple provides a spiritual stillness in the middle of a world in chaos, "a place of refuge" (Isaiah 4:6) for the covenant seeker and keeper. Elder Bednar taught that "in His holy house, if we will, we can be still and know that God is our Heavenly Father, we are His children, and Jesus Christ is our Savior." In times of turmoil and unrest, we can be blessed by the spiritual stillness that comes from Christ-centered hope, which "cometh of faith, and maketh an anchor to the souls of men" (Ether 12:4). When our hope is focused on the Savior and our temple covenants that bind us to Him, there is no movement of the earth, or the temporal world, that can shake us. Our covenants, and our faith in Him, become our ninety-eight base isolators to keep us protected from temporal tremors and their associated agitation and displacement. Elder Bednar described this as a "higher and holier dimension of stillness in our lives—an inner spiritual stillness of the soul."[18] The Salt Lake Temple renovation illuminates the value and importance of stillness in a real-world application.

The effect of the base isolators in disconnecting the temple from the earth could also be compared to President Russell M Nelson's teaching to overcome the world. He asked:

> What does it mean to overcome the world? . . . It means trusting the doctrine of Christ more than the philosophies of men. . . . [It is] not an event that happens in a day or two. It happens over a lifetime as we repeatedly embrace the doctrine of Christ. . . . Spend more time in the temple, and seek to understand how the temple teaches you to rise above this fallen world.[19]

The base isolators, in a very real sense, allow the temple itself to rise above this fallen world, just as binding ourselves to the Savior through temple covenants allows us to view ourselves in our own carnal state (see Mosiah 4:2) and thus rise above our fallen state (see Mosiah 16:5).

President Nelson reinforced this truth when discussing the Salt Lake Temple's foundation during his October 2021 General Conference address: "Please believe me when I say that when your spiritual foundation is built solidly upon Jesus Christ, you have no need to fear. As you are true to your covenants made in the temple, you will be strengthened by His power. Then, *when spiritual earthquakes occur, you will be able to stand strong because your spiritual foundation is solid and immovable.*"[20]

Notes

1. "Remarks by President Brigham Young," *Deseret News*, Oct. 14, 1893, 97. Also found in Brigham Young, *Journal of Discourses*, 10:254. See also, R. Scott Lloyd, "Church History Set in Quarry's Stone," *Church News*, Oct. 4, 2003.
2. Journal History, October 9, 1852, 1. As quoted in Jacob W. Olmstead, Josh Probert, and Elwin C. Robison, "Myths and Realities of the Salt Lake Temple Foundation," *Journal of Mormon History* 48, no. 4 (2022): 32–65, https://doi.org/10.5406/24736031.48.4.02.
3. Brigham Young was a self-described "chemist in theory" and held the pseudoscientific opinion that the pyramids had been built of a type of mud brick. He further believed that adobe would become harder over time and that using this material would create the most long-lasting temple possible, as was evidenced, in his mind, by the longevity of the pyramids. Brigham Young, in *Journal of Discourses*, 1:218–20.
4. Brigham Young, in *Journal of Discourses*, 1:218–20.
5. He then said that "if it is built of San Pete rock [oolite], when he looks down to see it he will find it ain't there, but it is gone, washed into the Jordan. It cannot remain, it must decay." Brigham Young, in *Journal of Discourses*, 1:220.
6. Jacob W. Olmstead, Josh Probert, and Elwin C. Robison, "Myths and Realities of the Salt Lake Temple Foundation," *Journal of Mormon History* 48, no. 4 (2022): 32–65, https://doi.org/10.5406/24736031.48.4.02.
7. Presiding Bishopric presentation on the Salt Lake Temple to the First Presidency, October 2015. As cited by Gary A. Stevenson, "A Good Foundation Against the Time to Come," *Ensign* or *Liahona*, May 2020, 49.
8. Stevenson, "A Good Foundation," 49.
9. Sarah Jane Weaver, "President Nelson Outlines Plans for Salt Lake Temple during Its Four-Year Closure for Renovation," *Church News*, Apr. 19, 2019.
10. Russell M. Nelson, "The Temple and Your Spiritual Foundation," *Liahona*, Nov. 2021, 93.
11. Olmstead et al., "Salt Lake Temple Foundation."
12. Tad Walch, "Moroni's Trumpet Fell One Year Ago. Where Is It Now and What's Happened Since?," *Deseret News*, Mar. 18, 2021.
13. Trent Toone, "Utah Earthquake Causes Angel Moroni on Salt Lake Temple to Lose His Trumpet," *Deseret News*, Mar. 18, 2020.

14. Adapted from "Salt Lake Temple and Temple Square Renovation Updates," The Church of Jesus Christ of Latter-day Saints, last modified Aug. 26, 2024, https://www.churchofjesuschrist.org/feature/templesquare/temple-square-construction-updates.
15. Scott Taylor, "What Is 'Jack and Bore' and How Is It Holding up the 187-Million-Pound Salt Lake Temple?," Aug. 26, 2022, https://www.thechurchnews.com/temples/2022/8/26/23323765/what-is-jack-and-bore-salt-lake-temple-renovation/.
16. All images come from "Salt Lake Temple and Temple Square Renovation Updates."
17. "Salt Lake Temple and Temple Square Renovation Updates."
18. David A Bednar, "Be Still, and Know That I Am God," *Liahona*, May 2024, 28.
19. Russell M. Nelson, "Overcome the World and Find Rest," *Liahona*, Nov. 2022, 96–98.
20. Russell M. Nelson, "The Temple and Your Spiritual Foundation," *Liahona*, Nov. 2021, 95; emphasis added.

About the Authors

Kenneth L. Alford is a professor of Church history and doctrine at Brigham Young University and a retired US Army colonel.

Jeanne W. Anderson is the great-great-granddaughter of James Campbell Livingston and Hannah Widdison Livingston.

Susan Easton Black is an emeritus professor of Church history and doctrine at Brigham Young University.

Leah Darby recently graduated from at Brigham Young University majoring in editing and publishing with a minor in French.

Richard O. Cowan is an emeritus professor of Church history and doctrine at Brigham Young University.

Alonzo L. Gaskill is a professor of Church history and doctrine at Brigham Young University.

Maclane E. Heward is an assistant professor of Church history and doctrine at Brigham Young University.

Scott L. Howell is an assistant teaching professor of Church history and doctrine at Brigham Young University.

Emily Lambert is originally from the San Francisco Bay Area and is a student at Brigham Young University, studying viola performance.

Sam LeFevre is married, the father of four daughters, and grandfather of ten grandchildren. He recently retired after a forty-year career in public health. Sam served in the Salt Lake Temple from 2009 until its closing in 2019 and is now serving in the Bountiful Utah Temple.

Mark D. Ogletree is a professor of Church history and doctrine at Brigham Young University.

Craig James Ostler is an emeritus professor of Church history and doctrine at Brigham Young University.

Derek R. Sainsbury is an associate professor of Church history and doctrine at Brigham Young University.

Andrew C. Skinner is an emeritus professor of ancient scripture at Brigham Young University.

James Smith is an associate professor of civil and construction engineering at Brigham Young University.

Seth G. Soha is a graduate of Brigham Young University and an independent researcher in the field of religious studies. He is also a board-certified physician assistant with an established practice in the state of Utah.

Milton Richard Walker and Kathryn Hinckley Barnes Walker served as the Salt Lake Temple president and matron from 2005 to 2008.

Mike Winder was Ned Winder's grandson, next-door neighbor, and biographer. Mike is the author of fourteen published books, including his latest work, *Hidden in Hollywood: The Gospel Found in 1001 Movie Quotes*.

B. Jackson and Rosemary M. Wixom served as the president and matron of the Salt Lake Temple from November 2017 to December 2019.

Mary Jane Woodger is a professor of Church history and doctrine at Brigham Young University.

Trevor Wylie lives in Tooele, Utah, with wife, Melia, and six kids. He is the manager of preservation imaging at the Church History Library and holds degrees from Brigham Young University and San Jose State University.